I0867577

CHRIS BRAITHWAITE

Mariner, Renegade, & Castaway

CHRIS BRAITHWAITE
Mariner, Renegade, & Castaway

Seafarers' Organizer, Socialist, and Militant Pan-Africanist

Christian Høgsbjerg

On Our Own Authority! Publishing
Atlanta, Georgia

Chris Braithwaite: Mariner, Renegade, & Castaway

by Christian Høgsbjerg.

Copyright © 2017

On Our Own Authority! Publishing.
Atlanta, Georgia.

All rights reserved. This book may not be reproduced in any form by any electronic or mechanical means including photocopying, recording, or information storage and retrieval without permission in writing from the author and publisher.

ISBN-13: 978-0-9906418-6-5
ISBN-10: 0-9906418-6-4
LCCN: 2017906924

www.oooabooks.org
oooabooks@gmail.com

First published with the Socialist History Society (Occasional Publication 33), in association with Redwords book in 2014

Cover design by Julia Simoniello and Andrew Zonneveld

Chris Braithwaite, aged about 55, c. 1940
(Photo courtesy of his family)

CONTENTS

ACKNOWLEDGMENTS

With very special thanks to Marika Sherwood, and also to Chris Braithwaite's family, particularly Jeannette Alade, Angela Oritsejafor and Dorothy Rose du Boulay. I would like to also thank Talat Ahmed, Gaverne Bennett, Ian Birchall, Barbara Bush, Sally Campbell, David Featherstone, David Goodway, John Griffiths, David Howell, Roger Huddle, Hassan Mahamdallie, David Morgan, Matthew Quest, Chris Searle, and Dan Whittall. I am grateful to have been given the chance to talk on Braithwaite at the conference "'Salty' Geographies: Subaltern maritime networks, spaces and practices," held at the University of Glasgow in October 2010, and also at a seminar and then the annual conference of the Black and Asian Studies Association in London in 2011. I have written briefer biographical sketches of Braithwaite for *Race & Class* (Vol. 53, No. 2, October, 2011), the *Black and Asian Studies Newsletter* (No. 60, 2011), *The Palgrave Encyclopedia of Imperialism and Anti-Imperialism* (2015), and the *Dictionary of Caribbean and Afro-Latin American Biography* (2016), and I am indebted to the editors of those publications for their support. Finally, I would like to thank the Harry Ransom Humanities Research Center, University of Texas at Austin for providing me with reports by Nancy Cunard from 1941 and 1943, and for granting me permission to quote from them, and I also remain grateful for the support of the Chris Braithwaite Estate. For this new edition, I am indebted to the work of Andrew Zonneveld and the wider team at OOOA Books. The text remains essentially the same as in the first edition, with a few very minor revisions and the inclusion of one or two new details about Braithwaite's remarkable life that have come to light since 2014.

Christian Høgsbjerg, 2017.

INTRODUCTION

In 1945, the British socialist and feminist novelist Ethel Mannin, a "determined collector of 'interesting people,'" penned a satirical novel, *Comrade O Comrade*, in which she reminisced about the politics of the British far-Left during the 1930s.[1] Subtitled "Low-down on the Left," Mannin noted that "not all the characters in this story are entirely fictitious." "'The distinguished colored Trotskyist' is recognizable to those who know the Left intimately" – it was a portrait of the black Trinidadian historian and writer C.L.R. James – but "the Negro socialist who turns up at various meetings will also be recognised by some people."

> He died not long ago, and the socialist and anti-imperialist struggle lost a valiant fighter by his death, and many of us,

1 R.F. Foster, *W.B. Yeats: a life*, Vol. II: the arch-poet, 1915-1939 (Oxford, Oxford University Press, 2003), p. 511. On Mannin, see Andy Croft, "Ethel Mannin: the red rose of love and the red flower of liberty," in Angela Ingram and Daphne Patai (eds.), *Rediscovering Forgotten Radicals: British women writers, 1889-1939* (Chapel Hill, University of North Carolina Press, 1993) and Robert Huxter, *Reg and Ethel: Reginald Reynolds (1905-1958), his life and work and his marriage to Ethel Mannin (1900-1984)* (York, Sessions, 1992).

> myself included, a good comrade and friend. I am quite certain that he would not merely not have minded my short caricatures of him in this book, but, on the contrary, feel flattered.[2]

This figure first appeared in the novel speaking on a platform alongside the famous veteran anarchist Emma Goldman at a rally in London held in solidarity with the Spanish Revolution:

> He had an enormous voice, an impassioned desire to secure justice and freedom for his oppressed people in Africa, a contempt for the Communists, and an unabounded admiration for Mary Thane [a character who was chairing the meeting, loosely based on Ethel Mannin herself] [...] The Negro loved speaking; he loved haranguing the crowd. He was in his element. He had five hundred and more people ranged in rows before him. It was a superb opportunity to put the anti-Imperialist case, with special reference to Africa. "Does he know this is a meeting about *Spain*, dear?" "Red Emma" twanged bitterly into Mary's ear. Mary made frantic efforts to pass a time-up note to the Negro, but he was in a river of rhetoric, a torrent of words, in full spate, and nothing short of a blow over the head would have stopped him. He [...] went on for a solid hour before reaching his final peroration. Then, covered with sweat and triumph, and amid prolonged applause, he came round to the back of the table and shook Mary by the hand, grinning hugely. This intensified the applause and he turned and bowed to the audience before seating himself. He was fine, Mary thought, passionately sincere in the fight for his oppressed people, only – only

2 Ethel Mannin, *Comrade O Comrade: or, Low-down on the left* (London, Jarrolds, 1947), p. 5. On C.L.R. James's life and work in the 1930s, see Christian Høgsbjerg, *C.L.R. James in Imperial Britain* (Durham, NC, Duke University Press, 2014).

> [...] it just didn't happen to be a meeting about British Imperialism...[3]

The unnamed black radical orator whose performance on the platform alongside Emma Goldman found its way into fictional form here was the Barbadian agitator and organizer Chris Braithwaite (1885-1944), better known under his adopted pseudonym "Chris Jones." Chris Braithwaite, as chair of the Colonial Seamen's Association (CSA), was perhaps the critical lynchpin of an anti-colonial maritime network in and around the imperial metropolis of inter-war London. It was during the 1930s when briefly in and around the Communist Party of Great Britain (CPGB), and then in militant Pan-Africanist organisations such as the International African Friends of Abyssinia [Ethiopia] (IAFA) and the International African Service Bureau (IASB) led by the outstanding black Trinidadian socialists George Padmore and C.L.R James, that Braithwaite's talents as an anti-imperialist and anti-capitalist activist came to the fore. Braithwaite's dedication to the cause of black and white unity and struggle from below against oppression and exploitation meant he came to the attention of the British state as early as 1930, when Stephen Howe notes that he was regarded by one undercover police officer as "the CP's most valuable contact among colonial seamen."[4] Scholars of militant anti-colonialism have long acknowledged his status as "one of the leading black activists in Britain in the 1930s," to quote Jonathan Derrick.[5]

---

3 Mannin, *Comrade O Comrade*, p. 118. Mannin's partner, the anti-imperialist writer Reginald Reynolds describes in his 1956 memoir how this account of a rally on Spain in which both Goldman and Braithwaite spoke was based on a real meeting. See Reginald Reynolds, *My Life and Crimes* (London, Jarrolds, 1956), pp. 153-54. In 1941, Mannin published *Red Rose*, a novel about Emma Goldman, while for more on Goldman and her meetings on the Spanish Revolution in London, see David Goodway, *Anarchist Seeds Beneath the Snow: left-libertarian thought and British writers from William Morris to Colin Ward* (Liverpool, Liverpool University Press, 2006), pp. 125, 132-34.

4 See the "Secret Report on Communist Party Activities in Great Britain among Colonials" submitted to the Colonial Office by Superintendent E. Parket on 22 April 1930, quoted in Stephen Howe, *Anticolonialism in British Politics: The left and the end of empire, 1918-1964* (Oxford, Clarendon Press, 1993), p. 86.

5 Jonathan Derrick, *Africa's "Agitators": militant anti-colonialism in Africa and the West,*

Despite such formal recognition in the scholarly literature, Braithwaite still remains a distinctly overlooked if not almost completely forgotten figure, particularly in the wider collective memory of black British radicalism and black internationalism more generally.[6] This booklet will attempt to go some way towards remedying this situation by providing a long overdue biographical portrait of this black radical Caribbean activist, a clearly outstanding figure in the rich, "hidden history" of not only black British radicalism, but also the twentieth-century revolutionary black and red Atlantic.[7] Such an undertaking of historical recovery and retrieval would not have been possible without the often pioneering research on Braithwaite's life and work that has already been undertaken by historians such as Marika Sherwood, Hakim Adi and Barbara Bush.[8] I am also greatly indebted to

---

1918-1939 (London, Hurst & Company, 2008), p. 284.

6 One reason for this is that, the CPGB aside, almost all of the radical political organizations with which Braithwaite was involved, including the IAFA, the IASB and particularly the CSA itself, still await serious scholarly attention as radical political organisations. For my development of this argument, see Christian Høgsbjerg, "Black Books," *History Workshop Journal*, 70 (2010), a review of Carol Polsgrove's important and insightful work on the Pan-Africanists around George Padmore from the 1930s to the 1950s, which has only one passing reference to Braithwaite. See Carol Polsgrove, *Ending British rule in Africa: writers in a common cause* (Manchester, Manchester University Press, 2009), p. 45. For other works which have little on Braithwaite himself, but remain valuable introductions for contextualizing the experience and contribution of some of his more illustrious contemporaries, see Brent Hayes Edwards, *The Practice of Diaspora; literature, translation, and the rise of black internationalism* (London, Harvard University Press, 2003), Leslie James, *George Padmore and Decolonization from Below: Pan-Africanism, the Cold War, and the End of Empire* (Basingstoke: Palgrave, 2015), Bill Schwarz, (ed.), *West Indian Intellectuals in Britain* (Manchester, Manchester University Press, 2003) and Satnam Virdee, Racism, *Class and the Racialized Outsider* (London: Palgrave Macmillan, 2014).

7 For a popular introduction to "black British radicalism," see Hassan Mahamdallie, *Black British Rebels: Figures from Working Class History* (London, Bookmarks, 2012).

8 Given the Special Branch file on Chris Braithwaite seems, like that kept on George Padmore, to have been "accidentally destroyed," I am particularly indebted to Marika Sherwood for her support for my research on Braithwaite and for kindly sharing her own personal research "file" on Braithwaite with me, which included George Padmore's obituary and Braithwaite's own writings for *International African Opinion*, collected in the appendices.

Chris Braithwaite's family, some of whom I have had the honor of meeting after presenting my research on Braithwaite to the Black and Asian Studies Association, for their kind support for this project and for generously sharing information about their family with me. Here I would like to particularly thank Dorothy Rose du Boulay, who had already undertaken her own research about her grandfather and who kindly consented to share some of this and her own thoughts with an outsider like myself. This booklet makes no pretence to be a full biographical study of Chris Braithwaite, which would require many more years of archival work and research. It does however aim to make a small contribution towards the writing of what the great Marxist maritime historian Marcus Rediker has called "a people's history of the sea."[9] It locates what is known of Braithwaite's life and work within the wider collective struggle of radical black colonial seafarers. They resisted oppression and exploitation in the British shipping industry and in the imperial metropolis itself, and also helped enable militant Pan-Africanist organizations to establish networks of resistance throughout the colonial world.

9 Marcus Rediker, "Towards a people's history of the sea," in David Killingray, Margarette Lincoln and Nigel Rigby (eds.) *Maritime Empires: British Imperial Maritime Trade in the Nineteenth Century* (Woodbridge, The Boydell Press, 2004).

BLACK BARBADIAN MARINER

Christopher M. Braithwaite was born in the British West Indian colony of Barbados in 1885.[1] His grandfather had been enslaved, but had remarkably taught himself to read the Bible and both his mother and father had also been literate.[2] This was not so unusual for Barbados: historian Winston James has (perhaps a little provocatively) written of "the superior cultural capital" of many Barbadians compared to the rest of the Caribbean, arguing that "from the eighteenth century, Barbadians have been among the most literate and educated black population in the world."[3] Doubtless, Chris's parents encouraged their son to read the classics of English literature. His father was a disciplinarian, and this perhaps helps explain Chris's early aspirations to join the police or train to be a lawyer. However, after school, around the

1 The 1944 register in Stepney of Braithwaite's death lists his full name and year of birth. George Padmore, "Chris Jones: fighter for the oppressed," *New Leader*, 23 September 1944, reprinted in Appendix B.

2 Interview with Dorothy Rose du Boulay, 24 June 2011.

3 Winston James, *Holding Aloft the Banner of Ethiopia: Caribbean radicalism in early twentieth-century America* (London, Verso, 1999), p. 118.

time he was 17 or 18, Chris, for reasons that are still unclear, decided to leave home and run away to sea.[4]

It is worth noting here that Chris's early life in Barbados would have been lived in the context of a severe economic depression on the island, sparked by falling European sugar prices (caused by an increase in subsidised domestic sugar beet production) in the 1880s. This economic crisis would last until the First World War (when many sugar beet zones in Europe were destroyed). As Hilary Beckles notes, wage-cutting by planters in Barbados created "social unrest among the increasingly impoverished labouring poor [...] evidence of rising mortality and general malnutrition caused much concern to law-enforcing agents."[5] Starvation was not uncommon, and "food scavenging was the order of the day." In 1895, for example, a "potato raid" took place on several plantations, "a form of praedial larceny in which workers expressed the ideological notion of 'justified appropriation.'" Outbreaks of typhoid and dysentery and a smallpox epidemic added to the rising death toll among the poor, and in 1910 a medical officer noted that "chronic pauperism [...] like a chronic disease is [...] undermining the population of this island."[6]

Indeed, by the early twentieth century, the tiny island of Barbados was perhaps the hardest hit out of all the Caribbean islands by the general crisis of "over-population" and poverty wages resulting from the catastrophic decline of the sugar industry. As Winston James notes, "after Jamaica, Barbados was the major source of Caribbean emigration in the late nineteenth and early twentieth centuries [...] Barbados disgorged 150,000 of its sons and daughters between 1861 and 1921, a figure equivalent to the entire population of the island in 1861."[7] Chris Braithwaite was then one among the tens of thousands who left Barbados. His friend and comrade from the 1930s onwards, George Padmore, has left us perhaps as full an account as we are ever likely to get of Braithwaite's new life, working as a seafarer:

4 Interview with Dorothy Rose du Boulay, 24 June 2011.

5 Hilary McD. Beckles, *A History of Barbados: From Amerindian settlement to nation-state* (Cambridge, Cambridge University Press, 1990), p. 132.

6 Beckles, *A History of Barbados*, pp. 138, 140.

7 James, *Holding Aloft the Banner of Ethiopia*, p. 30. See also Mary Chamberlain, *Empire and nation-building in the Caribbean: Barbados, 1937-66* (Manchester, Manchester University Press, 2010), pp. 26-50.

> Chris [...] started to go to sea at the very early age. As a seaman he had the opportunity to travel round the world. The world was thus his university, and what an education it provided him! It was always a pleasure to hear Chris, who was of a most gay and youthful temperament, relate his many sailor's yarns, and, in his more serious moments, to listen to him describing the conditions of the working-class in the various lands it was his good fortune to visit.[8]

Some idea of the kind of "education" the young black Barbadian mariner might have gained while travelling the world at a time when white supremacy so flagrantly and blatantly dominated under the flags of competing European empires can be guessed at from one piece of autobiographical writing by another young Caribbean migrant born in 1887, not long after Braithwaite, who also travelled around the world – the Jamaican Pan-Africanist Marcus Garvey. At eighteen, said Garvey,

> I started to take an interest in the politics of my country, and then I saw the injustice done to my race because it was black, and I became dissatisfied on that account I went travelling to South and Central America and parts of the West Indies to find out if it was so elsewhere, and I found the same situation. I set sail for Europe to find out if it was different there, and again I found the same stumbling block – "You are black."[9]

Braithwaite also encountered what the great black American radical historian W.E.B. Du Bois would call "the problem of the colour line." In a speech he gave in 1941, Braithwaite declared that for "forty years he has been a rolling stone in every part of the world [...] he had yet to find a spot

8 Padmore, "Chris Jones."

9 Quoted in James, *Holding Aloft the Banner of Ethiopia*, p. 71. Braithwaite's relationship to Garveyism requires further research.

where under white domination elementary freedom is granted to the subject races."[10]

The British merchant navy, where Braithwaite found employment, was, alongside cotton textiles, shipbuilding, and coal, one of the staple industries of British capitalism.[11] By the turn of the century growing international competition had led to cheaper colonial labor being increasingly employed, and young black seafarers were recruited in huge numbers. Much shipping was freight, sometimes especially long voyages on "tramp" ships, and colonial seafarers were, as Laura Tabili notes, "a labour reserve filling the least desirable and least steady jobs," such as firemen and stoking the coal, particularly tough work in often unbearable heat.[12] Jonathan Hyslop has described labor conditions in the engine room on steamships:

> The engine room housed the great furnaces that produced the energy to power the ship. The main types of labourers here were the "trimmers" who brought the coal forward from the bunkers in which it was kept towards the furnaces, and the firemen who shovelled the fuel into the furnaces and ensured that they burned at the right temperatures. The engine room was an industrial hell. Trimmers and firemen were in constant danger of being burned by the furnaces, crushed by sliding coal, choked by dust, smoke and fumes, or overcome by heat exhaustion.[13]

10 *New Leader*, 23 August 1941.

11 As Avner Offer has noted, during the period 1870-1914 the British mercantile marine was "by far the largest in the world, with about 35 percent of world tonnage throughout the period [1870-1914] (and another 5-9 percent in British possessions)...British trade and investment built up the demand for ships, and provided them with cargoes." Avner Offer, "Costs and Benefits, Prosperity, and Security, 1870-1914," in Andrew Porter (ed.), *The Oxford History of the British Empire, Vol. III, The Nineteenth Century* (Oxford, Oxford University Press, 1999), p. 696.

12 Laura Tabili, *"We Ask for British Justice:" Workers and racial difference in late imperial Britain* (London, Cornell University Press, 1994), pp. 3, 39.

13 Jonathan Hyslop, "Steamship Empire: Asian, African and British Sailors in the Merchant Marine c. 1880-1945," *Journal of Asian and African Studies* (Vol. 44, No. 1, 2009), p. 56.

The luckier laborers on a steamship worked on deck or in the saloon, helping prepare the food. Yet while employed in the merchant navy, it seems Braithwaite, like many sailors, developed the habits of the autodidactic, finding time to read. As one friend and comrade of his from the 1930s onwards, the anti-imperialist writer and activist Reginald Reynolds - the partner of Ethel Mannin - recalled, Braithwaite, "a very dark Negro [...] of medium height, thick-set and engagingly ugly," had "received very little schooling but he had seen the world in the merchant service, read a little, thought a lot and made up his mind on all major issues."[14]

After several years, Braithwaite moved to settle in America. He took up residence in Chicago, Illinois, which by the early twentieth century had emerged as the second city of the United States. Mainly as a result of the "Great Migration" of black Americans from the South then under way, Chicago had a small and steadily growing black population in the South Side area of the city. Braithwaite had a relationship with a black American woman and fathered six sons.[15] That many Caribbean workers like Braithwaite settled in the United States in the early twentieth century despite the Jim-Crow laws and harsh racism is not so surprising, and the apparent freedoms of America compared to the experience of British colonialism in the Caribbean ensured it was the most common destination for West Indian migrants. Between 1899 and 1931, over one hundred thousand Caribbean-born people had made just such a move.[16] As C.L.R. James noted in 1938, the U.S. was "the Mecca of all West Indian Negroes before the slump."[17] For example, James's

14 Reynolds, *My Life and Crimes*, p. 118. That Braithwaite had reputedly read widely while employed in the merchant navy was confirmed by Mannin in later correspondence with Barbara Bush. Barbara Bush, *Imperialism, Race and Resistance: Africa and Britain, 1919-1945* (London, Routledge, 1999), p. 222.

15 Interview with Dorothy Rose du Boulay, 24 June 2011. On the black population of Chicago in this period, see for example Allan H. Spear, *Black Chicago: The Making of a Negro Ghetto, 1890-1920* (Chicago, University of Chicago Press, 1967).

16 Chamberlain, *Empire and nation-building in the Caribbean*, p. 28. There is extensive discussion of Caribbean migration to America in James's *Holding Aloft the Banner of Ethiopia.*

17 C.L.R. James, *A History of Negro Revolt* (London, Fact, 1938), p. 67.

childhood friend Malcolm Nurse (George Padmore) would make the move from Trinidad to the US in 1924.[18]

The early years of the twentieth century were, as Winston James notes, "dark times for black America:"

> During the first two decades of the century, lynching was commonplace and generally passed unpunished in the South. This was the era of Booker T. Washington's hegemony, the era of black accommodationism, timid obsequiousness before the powers that be, albeit conditioned by formidable circumscription.[19]

What Braithwaite made of the high levels of institutionalized racism in Chicago remain unknown, nor is it known what kind of relationship, if any, he had to the working class militants embodying the city's radical political traditions which had, for example, helped to give birth in 1905 to the Industrial Workers of the World (IWW). Many Caribbean migrants to America were attracted by the Wobblies, as the IWW were known, including such leading black radical intellectuals as Hubert Harrison and Claude McKay. The IWW's anti-racism, internationalism and commitment to organizing all workers, regardless of skill, color, sex, or national origin also won it the respect of many black Caribbean workers, particularly in Philadelphia where a significant number of black longshoremen joined the Marine Transport Workers Industrial Union, Local 8 of the IWW.[20]

---

18 As James remembered, "Padmore shook the dust of the cramping West Indies from his feet in the early 1920s and went to the United States." C.L.R. James, *The Black Jacobins: Toussaint L'Ouverture and the San Domingo revolution* (London, Penguin, 2001), p. 310.

19 James, *Holding Aloft the Banner of Ethiopia*, p. 94.

20 James, *Holding Aloft the Banner of Ethiopia*, p. 183. For more on Local 8 of the IWW Maritime Transport Workers Union, see David Featherstone, *Solidarity: Hidden Histories and Geographies of Internationalism* (London, Zed Books, 2012), pp. 83-87. On the IWW and black workers, see also Ahmed Shawki, *Black Liberation and Socialism* (Chicago, Haymarket, 2006), pp. 124-128.

Braithwaite, the "rolling stone," at some point decided to return to the sea, leaving his new family in Chicago.[21] The British merchant navy was particularly dependent on the labor of colonial seafarers during the Great War as white British seafarers were conscripted to the Royal Navy.[22] According to a 1943 interview Braithwaite gave to the radical poet, editor, publisher, and journalist Nancy Cunard, he worked during the Great War as "chief donkey-man," a responsible job involving ensuring the maintenance of the "donkey-engines'" used on ships to drive windlasses, the winches, the cranes and such machinery. Once again, he "sailed the seven seas."[23]

After the war, Braithwaite returned to America - though not it seems this time to Chicago - and according to Cunard instead worked for a period "in a New York bar."[24] The "black Mecca" of New York was a popular destination for Caribbean migrant workers like Braithwaite though the horrifically high levels of racism in America remained a critical issue. As Mary Chamberlain notes, while New York's "existing Caribbean social networks, originating in the nineteenth century, provided opportunities for accommodation, support and employment," migrants from the black majority societies of the Caribbean "entered a society profoundly divided by race, and in ways new to West Indians."[25] Yet Braithwaite would not have felt too alone in New York for, as Winston James notes, "among the black migrants to New York were thousands of mariners."[26]

---

21 It is not known what happened to Braithwaite's six sons.

22 "The advent of war had led to a considerable increase in the number of black (lascar and British) and Chinese seamen on British ships. When war was declared, 8,000 merchant seamen joined the armed forces, while a further 9,000 nationals of now hostile countries were sacked. Black workers were among those who replaced them, particularly during 1915-17 when wages were increased and labour was recruited in the colonies themselves." Paul Gordon and Danny Reilly, "Guestworkers of the sea: racism in British shipping," *Race & Class* (Vol. 28, No. 2, 1986), p. 75.

23 Nancy Cunard, "On the coloured seamen in the Merchant Navy," report submitted to the Ministry of Information in June 1943, p. 1, Folder 1.3, Nancy Cunard Collection, Harry Ransom Humanities Research Center, University of Texas at Austin.

24 Cunard, "On the coloured seamen in the Merchant Navy," p. 1.

25 Chamberlain, *Empire and nation-building in the Caribbean,* p. 29.

26 James, *Holding Aloft the Banner of Ethiopia*, p. 71.

Many black Caribbean mariners settled in the United States, and some became leading radical militants in the American working class movement like Ferdinand Smith, the Jamaican born co-founder of the National Maritime Union and the equally remarkable figure of Hugh Mulzac, born on Union Island in the Grenadines, who after traveling to New York from Barbados worked for a period as a ship captain on Marcus Garvey's Black Star Line.[27] In New York, it seems likely Braithwaite would have witnessed, and possibly also participated in, the mass harbor strike of October 1919, which Calvin Winslow describes as "perhaps the largest harbour strike ever," and which closed 700 miles of waterfront, stranded 650 ships and involved possibly 150,000 workers and which lasted for over a month before ultimate defeat.[28]

> Forty to seventy thousand longshoremen struck – it was agreed it was impossible accurately to estimate the size of this vast waterfront workforce. The longshoremen were then joined by tens of thousands of others, workers from dozens of harbour trades ... the strike was a bold adventure, a remarkable display of industrial power. It involved virtually every longshoreman who worked in the Harbour, uniting Irish and Italians, blacks, Hungarians, Swedes, Russians. It effectively stopped shipping for nearly one month ...[29]

27 On Ferdinand Smith and the NMU, see Gerald Horne, *Red Seas: Ferdinand Smith and radical black sailors in the United States and Jamaica* (London, New York University Press, 2005), which also discusses Mulzac, among other things author of an autobiographical "classic work of proletarian literature," *A Star to Steer By*. On Mulzac, as well as Hugh Mulzac, *A Star to Steer By* (Berlin, Seven Seas Books, 1965), see George Padmore, "Negro sea captain," *Tribune*, 26 February 1943 and James, *Holding Aloft the Banner of Ethiopia*, pp. 92-3.

28 Calvin Winslow, "On the Waterfront: Black, Italian and Irish Longshoremen in the New York Harbour Strike of 1919," in John Rule and Robert Malcolmson (eds.) *Protest and Survival: Essays for E.P. Thompson* (London, Merlin, 1993), pp. 355, 361.

29 Winslow, "On the Waterfront," pp. 355, 359.

As Winslow notes, "new solidarities were constructed, and ethnic isolation diminished" during the New York Harbour Strike and the struggle for industrial unionism on the waterfront. "The rank-and-file character of the strike, and the degree to which the conflict was changing the consciousness of the strikers, was illustrated in a series of mass meetings." One black striker, Bell, got "more applause than any other" for his brief intervention from the floor in one such strike meeting:

> The Negro in New York is suffering more now than any other in the city. You don't know the high rentals imposed upon us in the Harlem section. It is really a disgrace. But let me tell you and the men in this hall that the Negro will stick with the men and do as they do.[30]

After a brief period of time spent in New York, Braithwaite crossed the Atlantic Ocean to make the "voyage in" to imperial Britain. For Braithwaite, now in his early-to-mid-thirties, this "voyage in" would prove a fateful one. Yet his subsequent political radicalization in Britain itself perhaps owed something to his previous experience of seeing the most intense and seemingly entrenched forms of racism confronted in the course of such mass class struggles as that which had brought the waterfront of New York to a standstill for a month. Certainly, he seems to have made himself a home of sorts while working in a bar in New York. When the African-American academic Ralph Bunche met the "very interesting" Braithwaite while in London in early 1937, he revealingly described him as coming "from Barbados and N.Y." in his diaries, and recorded that Braithwaite "thinks U.S. is the best country."[31]

30 Winslow, "On the Waterfront," pp. 356, 380, 382.

31 Susan D. Pennybacker, *From Scottsboro to Munich: race and political culture in 1930s Britain* (Oxford, Princeton University Press, 2009), p. 92.

FROM MARINER TO RENEGADE

In Britain, as Padmore noted, "Chris settled down in London as an employee of the Shipping Federation."[1] Braithwaite's work for the employers' Shipping Federation, based in London's Docklands, home to many black seafarers, was another highly respectable job. As a Shipping Federation agent in "the Pool," part of the River Thames where many ships come to dock, Braithwaite was responsible for finding and supplying colonial seafarers, engineers, stokers and others, often at a few hours notice. As he himself later told Nancy Cunard, he was "the only coloured man to have this as-a-rule white-man's job."[2] However, and quite remarkably given the relatively privileged job he had acquired, he soon immersed himself in the British working class movement and began to take politics more seriously. As Padmore recalled, after arriving in Britain Braithwaite took "an active part in the working-class struggles of this country, especially those affecting seamen – white as well as coloured."[3]

1 Padmore, "Chris Jones."

2 Cunard, "On the coloured seamen in the Merchant Navy," p. 1.

3 Padmore, "Chris Jones." C.L.R. James in a 1975 interview with Alan MacKenzie confirmed that Braithwaite's political radicalisation really dated from his settlement

Such political radicalization in the aftermath of the Great War in Britain was a common enough experience for black colonial seafarers, given the harsh conditions awaiting them in the recession-hit "Mother Country." As Laura Tabili notes in her important 1994 work on this experience in the interwar period, *'We Ask for British Justice,'* "the few thousand Black seamen living in Britain were only the most visible of a global and multiracial colonised population whose labour sustained Britain's imperial power." However, "the political economy of Britain's declining maritime empire created structural conditions conducive to conflict" in Britain itself.[4] The year 1919 of course had famously seen bloody race riots against ethnic minorities in nine British seaports - Glasgow, South Shields, Salford, Hull, London, Liverpool, Newport, Cardiff and Barry. Thousands of white British merchant seafarers had returned home from fighting in the Great War in search of employment to find not only housing shortages and the shipowners cutting wages but also a new level of competition for the few jobs available from black, Arab, Chinese and South Asian colonial seafarers. Many rallied to the slogan "Britishers first."[5] "British men for British ships" was another slogan raised, and this racist scapegoating was encouraged by the shipowners.[6]

Accordingly, Tabili writes that in British shipping, "interwar struggles were in part about efforts to 'expel' colonized people who had collectively and symbolically if not always personally entered the metropolitan workforce during the war."[7] The British state itself – through its Aliens control bureaucracy – ensured that the post war decline of British shipping was accompanied by a redefinition of British identity, a process that had

---

in Britain after the war. See Alan John MacKenzie, "British Marxists and the Empire: anti-imperialist theory and practice, 1920-1945," (unpublished Phd thesis, University of London, 1978), p. 180.

4 Tabili, *"We Ask for British Justice,"* pp. 2-3.

5 Jacqueline Jenkinson, *Black 1919; riots, racism and resistance in imperial Britain* (Liverpool, Liverpool University Press, 2009), p. 2. See also Neil Evans, "Across the universe: racial violence and the post-war crisis in imperial Britain, 1919-25," *Immigrants & Minorities* (Vol. 13, Nos. 2/3, 1994). This was a special issue of the journal edited by Diane Frost on "Ethnic Labour and British Imperial Trade: A History of Ethnic Seafarers in the UK."

6 Tabili, *"We Ask for British Justice,"* p. 111.

7 Tabili, *"We Ask for British Justice,"* pp. 11-12.

been accelerated by wartime xenophobia against Germans. Black and Asian colonial subjects had limited access to British passports, which as Tabili notes were "documents virtually unheard of for ordinary people before the war and unavailable in many parts of the empire" but "Alien's legislation" in 1919 and 1920 required "alien seamen" – in practice often undocumented black British colonial subjects – to register with local police if their stay ashore exceeded two months. In 1925, the Special Restriction (Coloured Alien Seamen) Order eliminated the 60-day grace period and so was "the first instance of state-sanctioned racial subordination inside Britain to come to widespread notice," "requiring all Black seamen in Britain's major ports to establish their British nationality or be registered as aliens."[8] Once registered as an "alien" with the police, black and Asian seafarers became liable to deportation from what for many, as colonial subjects, had been their "mother country."

By all accounts Braithwaite personally did not have any great reason or desire to stay in Britain anyway at this point, but this would change as a result of his relationship with and then marriage to Edna Slack, a young white woman originally from Derbyshire. They settled at 116 Turners Road near Stepney, an area in the East End of London in close proximity to the West India docks, and in 1929 would have their first child together, the first as it happened of six.[9] The support of white women in general would be often critical for black migrant workers, as marriage or cohabitation enabled black seafarers to claim domicile status and also entitlement to both better-paid work and relief.[10]

The fact that several thousand African and Caribbean seafarers like Braithwaite ultimately settled and founded households in Britain gave them an important advantage over say, the tens of thousands of Indian "Lascar."

8 Tabili, *"We Ask for British Justice,"* pp. 3, 35, 114, 120. See also Tony Lane, "The political imperatives of bureaucracy and empire: the case of the Coloured Alien Seamen Order, 1925," *Immigrants & Minorities* (Vol. 13, Nos. 2/3, 1994).

9 The address comes from correspondence between Nancy Cunard and Chris Braithwaite. Pamela, the baby girl born in 1929, was affectionately nicknamed "Dutchess," Harlem slang for "girl," as it was Chris's first daughter after having six sons from his previous relationship. Interview with Dorothy Rose du Boulay, 24 June 2011, and personal correspondence, 14 March 2013. Chris and Edna were married in 1936 in Stepney.

10 Tabili, *"We Ask for British Justice,"* pp. 140, 144. Bush, *Imperialism, Race and Resistance*, p. 222.

Arab or Chinese sailors who remained resident outside Britain, often in the colonies, and so only constituted temporary contract labor, with much reduced pay and conditions. Yet though black seafarers often managed to secure the "standard articles" given to white seafarers, they still held a fixed place below European seafarers in shipping's racial hierarchy.[11] More generally, as Baruch Hirson and Lorraine Vivian once noted, colonial sailors were "caught in a Catch 22 situation. Those who signed on at a colonial port were accused by British seamen of depressing wages while those who sought a berth in Britain [with a chance of better if not equal pay] ... were accused of depriving local men of jobs."[12] The National Union of Seamen (NUS), and its forerunner, the National Sailor's and Firemen's Union (NSFU), were complicit in the racially divisive practices fixing unequal pay in British shipping, and had cooperated closely with the employer's Shipping Federation in the state sanctioned National Maritime Board (NMB), set up during the Great War.[13] As Tabili notes, the NUS played a role "perpetuating the threat cheap labour constituted to men paid standard wages" while "'joint supply' boards composed of NMB affiliated unions' and owners' representatives would now control the distribution of jobs; [so] in practice sailors and firemen must join the NSFU to obtain employment."[14] Key to ensuring this took place was the introduction of a PC5 identification card for seafarers in 1921/22 – and so black seafarers like Braithwaite were forced to join the seafarers' union to get a PC5 card and so have any chance of finding work.[15]

Accordingly, as Tabili notes, "interwar practices in effect recolonised Black seamen in Britain, giving maritime employers privileged access to their labour." Though the need for a PC5 identification card led to the NSFU becoming "the first union to encounter significant numbers of black

---

11 See Tabili, *"We Ask for British Justice,"* p. 51.

12 Baruch Hirson and Lorraine Vivian, *Strike Across the Empire; the seamen's strike of 1925: in Britain, South Africa and Australasia* (London, Clio, 1992), p. 38. See also Tabili, *"We Ask for British Justice,"* p. 42.

13 See Marika Sherwood, "Race, nationality and employment among Lascar seamen, 1660-1945," *New Community*, 17/2 (1991), pp. 233-34.

14 Tabili, *"We Ask for British Justice,"* pp. 84, 93.

15 Arthur Marsh and Victoria Ryan, *The Seamen: a history of the National Union of Seamen, 1887-1987* (Oxford, Malthouse Press, 1989), p. 116.

workers" in Britain, the union itself actively colluded with the British state and shipowners to sustain racial barriers and reconstitute "imperial racial inequalities" in Britain itself. Racism tended to manifest itself with allusions to white English seafarers as a "maritime race" with "salt in the blood" in contrast to degenerate and dehumanised "tropical races."[16] "Englishmen," Braithwaite apparently once told Ralph Bunche privately in 1937, "are the most subtle g[od] d[amne]d prejudiced...people in the world."[17] Inside the NUS itself, an organization dominated during the 1920s by its overbearing leader Joseph Havelock Wilson, racial discrimination was also commonplace, part of a wider new discourse of what Jonathan Hyslop has called "white labourism" among the "imperial working class" in Britain.[18] As Tabili notes of the NUS, "repeated approaches by black union members seeking a voice in union governance were rebuffed."[19] Yet while Braithwaite - who seems to have been denied any kind of official position as a representative in the union - doubtless found such experiences disheartening, he pointed out the class dimensions of the widespread institutionalized racism. In 1938, for example, he stressed how racist ideas were continually reproduced as they fitted the employers' agenda of "Divide and Rule:"

> Colour discrimination is widespread in the marine industry, and it is exploited by the employers to play off one section of workers against the other. During my twenty years' membership of the Seamen's Union, I have often been confronted, like many African and West Indian seamen, with all kinds of racial chauvinism. Very frequently engineers would be willing to hire Negro seamen were it

16 Tabili, *"We Ask for British Justice,"* pp. 3, 55-7, 83-6. Padmore, "Chris Jones."

17 Quoted in Pennybacker, *From Scottsboro to Munich*, p. 92.

18 See Jonathan Hyslop, "The Imperial Working Class Makes Itself 'White': White Labourism in Britain, Australia, and South Africa Before the First World War," *Journal of Historical Sociology* (Vol. 12, No. 4, 1999).

19 Tabili, *"We Ask for British Justice,"* pp. 101-2. In 1929 "a petition from 'several coloured members of the Union in London' solicited the appointment of 'a coloured delegate ... to look after their interests.'" It seems almost certain Braithwaite was involved in this petition.

> not for the objection raised by some white seamen that "If you take the darkie, we will not sign on the ship."[20]

With such a clear perspective, it is not surprising that as George Padmore put it, "every progressive movement concerned with the welfare of seagoing folk" had the support of Braithwaite, even though, sadly, we currently know all too little about his union activism during the 1920s.[21] Indeed, we do not get our first real glimpse of Braithwaite the NUS militant until the summer of 1929, after the NUS itself had been temporarily expelled from the Trades Union Congress (TUC) for acting as a strikebreaking union during the 1926 General Strike. In a surviving letter that he wrote to the leadership of the union, Braithwaite reported "a very good and somewhat steamy chat with Jimmie Henson," who as Tabili notes was "a prominent NUS official temporarily estranged from the union and organising the Trades Union Congress [supported] Seamen's Section [of Ernest Bevin's Transport and General Workers' Union], a rival union."[22] Braithwaite reports of Henson that

> he stopped and spoke quietly then like a tornado, he let loose on me saying he never thought that I would assist at breaking up his meetings here in London … [and that] the Boys in Cardiff will tell me a thing or two when they hear that I helped to break up his meetings ... I got indignant at this remark. I told Henson if he wished me to, I will go to Cardiff tonight, or got to Hell with him or anyone who

20 Chris Jones, "Problems of coloured seamen," *International African Opinion*, I/1 (July, 1938). See Appendix A.

21 Padmore, "Chris Jones." We do not know, for example, whether he had any connection to the short-lived National African Sailors' and Firemen's Union (NASFU), based in Liverpool during the early 1920s, or how much of the rank-and-file seamen's militancy – which included an international wildcat strike in summer 1925 against a union-sanctioned pay cut – he took part in. On these, see Tabili, *"We Ask for British Justice,"* pp. 97, 157; Hirson and Vivian, *Strike Across the Empire.*

22 Letter dated 16 July 1929 from Chris Braithwaite to the NUS Temporary Management Committee, Warwick Modern Records Centre: MSS 175/328. Tabili, *"We Ask for British Justice,"* p. 81.

> can discredit me in the eyes of my colour, as I have done nothing to be ashamed of.[23]

Tabili suggests "the intensity of Braithwaite's retort" to a leading white trade unionist like Henson "perhaps reflected the painful choice he and other Black seamen faced, to join and support a union that subordinated and marginalized them or to remain even more vulnerable outside it." At best, and this statement remains a distinct understatement given the institutional racism which so afflicted the NUS, Tabili notes that "the story of the NUS and Black seamen is one of tragically missed opportunity:"

> The union fruitlessly pursued exclusion of the few thousand Black seamen in standard conditions of work, while colluding in the displacement of white and Black unionised seamen by growing numbers of super-exploited contract labourers. They rebuffed Black sailors' calls for union support and rejected overtures from colonial unions that might have forged an empirewide, thus global, labour movement to challenge continuing stratification.[24]

23 Letter dated 16 July 1929 from Braithwaite to the NUS Temporary Management Committee.

24 Tabili, *"We Ask for British Justice,"* pp. 82, 102-3. In 1934, the NUS Executive Committee refused to receive a deputation from the League Against Imperialism "with reference to the position of coloured seamen." This is testament to what David Featherstone has noted was "the reproduction of exclusionary forms of whiteness" by the NUS. See Featherstone, *Solidarity*, p. 73.

REVOLUTIONARY RENEGADE:
CHRIS BRAITHWAITE BECOMES CHRIS JONES

An attempt to build such an internationalist and multi-ethnic labor movement among seafarers during the 1920s was made by the Communist International (Comintern), formed in 1919 in the aftermath of the Russian Revolution. The Communist Party of Great Britain (CPGB) began to work towards organizing both white British and colonial seafarers through the Transport Workers Minority Movement and the National Minority Movement (NMM), formed in 1924 with Tom Mann as President. These two organizations were associated with the Profintern, the Red International of Labour Unions (RILU), based in Moscow. From 1928, and particularly following the Sixth World Congress of the Comintern that year, the importance of work among colonial seafarers was re-emphasised as a priority. That year, the leaders of the RILU had set up an International Trade Union Committee of Negro Workers (ITUC-NW) and the Transport Workers Minority Movement now made a special point of stressing that "Lascar [Indian], Chinaman, Arab or West Indian Negro" seafarers were not to blame for unemployment or low wages – and that "an injury to coloured seamen is a blow struck at British seamen."[1] However, this positive shift

1 Marika Sherwood, "The Comintern, the CPGB, colonies and black Britons, 1920-1938," *Science and Society*, 60/2 (1996), p. 152. For more context on the

and a renewed commitment to fighting any and every manifestation of "white chauvinism" took place within a wider destructive shift leftwards in the Comintern, a shift towards what were disastrously sectarian ultra-left politics. The distinctly catastrophist perspectives of "Third Period" Stalinism that now dominated the Comintern meant that a revolutionary situation was seen as not only emerging but declared to actually *exist* on a world scale. Bourgeois nationalists in colonial countries were fiercely denounced as collaborators with imperialism while in countries such as Britain social democracy was deemed to be "social fascism," the Labour Party and the trade unions declared to be an "auxiliary apparatus of the bourgeoisie," and so championing new breakaway "red" revolutionary trade unions was to become the order of the day.[2]

Accordingly, British delegates had also left the 1928 Comintern Congress committed to forming a new 'red' seafarers' union to counter the reactionary NUS. Though the Political Bureau of the CPGB in August 1928 agreed with this perspective, given "the fascist character of Wilson's [National] Union [of Seamen], [the] possibility of its expulsion from Swansea Trade Union Congress [the NUS was to be temporarily expelled from the TUC in 1928 for its role in the 1926 General Strike], [the] war danger and importance of seamen," they unanimously opposed forming a "new union for British seamen" in the here and now. This was not for any ideological reason but rather because "we had no organisation at all among seamen," and with only seven seafarers due to attend the CPGB national conference, to launch a new "red" union now would make the Party and Minority Movement "look ridiculous."[3] This was to remain the settled position of the CPGB, leading to well-documented tensions throughout the "Third Period," particularly

Communist International and its work among colonial seafarers in this period, see Hakim Adi, "The Comintern and black workers in Britain and France 1919-37," *Immigrants & Minorities*, 28/ 2-3 (2010). On the Profintern, see Reiner Tosstorff's massive history *The Red International of Labour Unions (RILU) 1920 - 1937* (Leiden, Brill, 2016), the first German edition of which was reviewed by Ian Birchall in *Historical Materialism*, 17/4 (2009).

2 James Eaden and David Renton, *The Communist Party of Great Britain since 1920* (Basingstoke, Palgrave, 2002), p. 36.

3 From a file in the James Klugmann papers at the Labour History Archive and Study Centre (LHASC) in Manchester's People's History Museum, LHASC: CP/IND/KLUG/05/01.

between the CPGB general secretary from 1929, Harry Pollitt, and various Comintern officials and agents, such as the seafarers' leader George Hardy, who, while apparently sceptical of "fixing dates" for the formation of a new "red" militant seafarers' union in Britain, tended to insist the forces which would allow such a process to take place were rapidly developing.[4]

However, in 1929, the CPGB did concretely work to build a new rank-and-file trade union grouping, the Seamen's Minority Movement (SMM), which soon established its own offices and a publication, *The Seafarer*. The SMM was led for the most part by George Hardy, who was elected honorary president of the new Hamburg-based International of Seamen and Harbour Workers (ISH) on its formation in 1930. Hardy's memoirs, *Those Stormy Years*, give a vivid recollection of the SMM's aims and objectives in inspiring a fightback over attacks on wages and conditions during the Great Depression, "as the employers tried to work off the cost of the crisis on to the workers' back."[5] As Stephen Howe notes, for the CPGB in terms of anti-colonial work, "apart from students – especially Indians [...] the most important source of possible contacts was thought to be colonial seamen in British ports. In 1930 it was reported that the party was working among them in Liverpool, Glasgow, South Wales, and London." The Communist writer Robin Page Arnot, author of a pamphlet on *How Britain Rules India* (1929), stressed the successes of this work. Speaking at a London CPGB meeting on 12 April 1930, Arnot noted the seafarer contacts the CPGB made "were generally willing to take literature and distribute it at foreign ports."[6]

---

4 George Hardy, *Those Stormy Years: Memories of the Fight for Freedom on Five Continents* (London, Lawrence and Wishart, 1956), pp. 217, 222-3. See also John Manley, "Moscow Rules? 'Red' Unionism and 'Class Against Class' in Britain, Canada and the United States, 1928-1935," *Labour/Le Trevail*, 56 (2005), pp. 9-49; Kevin Morgan, "The Trouble with Revisionism: or Communist History with the History Left In," *Labour/Le Trevail*, 63 (2009), pp. 131-155.

5 Hardy, *Those Stormy Years*, p. 215. On Hardy, see Andrew Flinn and Kevin Morgan, "George Hardy (1884-1966)," *Dictionary of Labour Biography*, XI (Basingstoke, Palgrave Macmillan, 2003), 98-109; Featherstone, *Solidarity*, pp. 83, 88; see also Hardy's Special Branch file at the National Archives (TNA) at Kew, London: TNA, KV2 / 1027 / 66.

6 Howe, *Anticolonialism and the British Left*, p. 66, quoting the previously mentioned "Secret Report on Communist Party Activities in Great Britain among Colonials."

Chris Braithwaite was one of those attracted towards the CPGB through the SMM, an affiliate of the ISH. He quickly seems to have realized the importance of adopting a pseudonym, "Chris Jones," to avoid victimization by his employer, the Shipping Federation. Braithwaite's experience as a NUS militant and the nature of his work made him an incredibly important recruit for the SMM. In April 1930 the NMM had set up a Colonial Committee and in November 1931 the SMM formed a committee of "militant coloured seamen." A Trinidadian seafarer, Jim Headley, who had been a ship's cook in the US (where he had been an activist in the radical National Maritime Union and the Young Communist League), had set up a International Seamen's Club (an "Interclub") in Poplar, a kind of social center for seafarers run with support and funding from the ISH. One "Chris Jones" chaired the second meeting of the "Committee of Coloured Seamen" of the SMM, a meeting attended by eleven blacks and three whites, which elected Headley to be its secretary. Other members of this Committee, which held its third meeting on 7 December 1931, included D. Benson, A. Semon and R. Kirkland. By late 1931 the leading African-American Communist James Ford could report to the ITUC-NW that "at Liverpool, Cardiff and London, Negro Comrades in cooperation with the SMM have been carrying out work among Negro seamen."[7] By 1931 if not before, Braithwaite had joined the CPGB itself, and "Chris Jones" was soon a leading member of the SMM, indeed a member of its central committee.[8]

---

7 Sherwood, "The Comintern, the CPGB, colonies and black Britons," p. 153, and RGASPI 534/5/223, folder 46-47 and RGASPI 534/5/223, folder 104, quoted in Holger Weiss, "The Hamburg Committee, Moscow and the Making of a Radical African Atlantic, 1930-1933, Part Two: The ISH, the IRH and the ITUCNW," *CoWoPA – Comintern Working Paper 20/2010* [online at the website of Åbo Akademi University], pp. 19-20. On Jim Headley, see Featherstone, *Solidarity*, pp. 90-91, and Headley's letter, "Let Us Close Ranks," to the *Negro Worker*, 2/7 (July 1932).

8 TNA, KV 2/1102/73a. One gets some sense of the everyday lives of black Communist seafarers in the East End of London in this period from the memoirs of Harold Rosen, then a young boy, who in his wonderful memoirs recalled his experience of meeting Jim Headley, and Headley's connections with Rosen's Jewish Communist grandparents, Joseph and Betsy Hyam. See Harold Rosen, *Are You Still Circumcised? East End Memories* (Nottingham, Five Leaves Publications, 1999), pp. 121-22, 124.

The CPGB's recruitment of Chris Braithwaite was an impressive gain, and he doubtless played a key role helping organize the international distribution of the officially banned "seditious" ITUC-NW publication the *Negro Worker* and other "Negro literature" into Africa and the Caribbean through his network of black colonial seafarers.[9] The ITUC-NW highlighted the injustices and appalling exploitation suffered by black seafarers internationally, but also showed that there was also resistance. In 1931, George Padmore – who had replaced Ford as head of the Hamburg-based ITUC-NW and now edited the *Negro Worker* - published his classic anti-imperialist work *The Life and Struggles of Negro Toilers*. An extract from it gives some flavour of the kind of politics motivating activists like Braithwaite in this period. Discussing the experience of West African seafarers from Liberia, Padmore noted:

> At various ports along the coast hundreds of men and boys belonging to the Kroc [sic] tribe are employed as stevedores, boatmen and sailors by European and American steamship companies operating in West Africa. The average wage of these marine workers is 20 to 24 cents per day of 12 hours. The following incident gives us an idea of the condition under which these black seamen are forced to work.
>
> "In 1924 fourteen Kroc [sic] boys complained that they had been unjustly imprisoned in Warri, a port in Nigeria, as a result of the complaint of a British captain, their employer, who charged that they had refused to obey his orders. The boys stated that they had been frequently compelled to work overtime from three o'clock in the morning to midnight - twenty-one of twenty-four hours; and that at Warri they had worked storing palm-oil from three o'clock one morning to one o'clock the following morning, when they were given permission to rest. At 2.45 a.m. they were ordered to scrub down the deck. At

9 See Hakim Adi, *Pan-Africanism and Communism: The Communist International, Africa and the Diaspora, 1919-1939* (Trenton, NJ, *Africa World Press*, 2013), p. 255. For more on the distribution of the *Negro Worker* by colonial seafarers, see Edwards, *The Practice of Diaspora*, pp. 258-9.

> the same time the captain upbraided them for having left three casks of oil on deck. The boys by this time 'began to jeer and to behave insolently,' whereupon the captain had them arrested and they were placed in a British prison while the steamer sailed away." (Buell: *Native Problem in Africa* Vol. II, Page 775).
>
> From time to time spontaneous strikes break out onboard ships, but these are invariably nipped in the bud largely because of the lack of organization and leadership.[10]

However, colonial seafarers remained a tiny fraction of the membership of the SMM during this period, and by February 1932, of the 1,000 odd members of the SMM only twenty-three were "colonials." Accordingly, in early 1932 Jim Headley wrote to his compatriot Padmore in Hamburg asking him "for a definite lead in order that the good work may be carried on." In April 1932, Padmore briefly visited London, and met Braithwaite when they both spoke at a meeting held at Poplar Town Hall organised by another Communist sponsored organization, International Labour Defence (ILD), in solidarity with the Scottsboro Boys.[11] The Scottsboro case saw nine black boys charged with the alleged rape of two white girls on a train in Alabama and all but the youngest boy facing the death penalty, and had dominated headlines internationally since March 1931.[12] Among the black Communists based in London, Braithwaite came to the fore in speaking out on the Scottsboro case, perhaps because, like Padmore himself, he had direct experience of racism in America. As Padmore recalled,

---

10 George Padmore, *Life and Struggles of Negro Toilers* (London, RILU ITUC-NW, 1931), pp. 71-72. Padmore's booklet also reported on a two month long seafarers' strike by Gambian sailors which sparked a general strike in 1930.

11 Sherwood, "The Comintern, the CPGB, colonies and black Britons," pp. 154-6. See also Pennybacker, *From Scottsboro to Munich,* p. 75. Padmore also apparently visited Liverpool. See Weiss, "The Hamburg Committee, Moscow and the Making of a Radical African Atlantic, 1930-1933, Part Two," p. 25.

12 See Haywood Patterson, *Scottsboro Boy* (London, Victor Gollancz, 1951), and James A. Miller, Susan D. Pennybacker, and Eve Rosenhaft, "Mother Ada Wright and the international campaign to free the Scottsboro Boys, 1931-1934," *American Historical Review* 106/2 (2001).

> I first met Chris about ten years ago. It was on the occasion of the mass meeting organised in London on behalf of the Scottsboro' boys, eight Negro youths who were being railroaded to death by American "justice." We were both speakers at that meeting, and from then a warm comradeship developed between us. Chris's participation in the endeavour to seek true justice for those Scottsboro' victims of class and race prejudice was typical of him. He never spared himself in rendering aid to the cause of the oppressed.[13]

If Padmore was impressed by Braithwaite, it is clear that Braithwaite was also equally impressed by Padmore, later praising him as "the greatest political leader of the Negroes in any part of the world."[14] The Comintern played a central role building defence campaigns around the Scottsboro case, and in Britain in 1931 a new militant anti-capitalist organization, the Negro Welfare Association (NWA), affiliated to the League Against Imperialism (LAI) and the ITUC-NW, threw itself into building solidarity action. The NWA, though not an exclusively black-led organisation, aimed "for the complete liberation and independence of all Negroes who are suffering from capitalist exploitation and imperialist domination," and was committed "to analyse, expose and combat capitalist exploitation and oppression in Africa, the West Indies, the other Negro colonies as well as in the USA."[15] According to Matthew Worley, the NWA was "formed on the initiative of two Afro-Caribbean communists, Arnold Ward and Chris Jones."[16] Arnold Ward, the NWA secretary, was a compatriot of Braithwaite's, and is another critical but

13 Padmore, "Chris Jones."

14 "Two Negro Leaders," *New Leader*, 23 August 1941.

15 Adi, *Pan-Africanism and Communism*, p. 259.

16 Matthew Worley, *Class Against Class: The Communist Party in Britain Between the Wars* (London, I.B. Taurus, 2002), p. 227. On Ward and the NWA, see Hakim Adi, "The Negro Question: The Communist International and Black Liberation in the Interwar Years," in Michael O. West, William G. Martin and Fanon Che Wilkins (eds), *From Toussaint to Tupac: the black international since the age of revolution* (Chapel Hill, University of North Carolina Press, 2009), pp. 167-8, 172.

overlooked figure in the history of radical Pan-Africanism in Britain. Born in Bridgetown, Barbados in 1886, Ward had resided in Trinidad and Germany (where he was interned as a British subject at the outbreak of the Great War) before being sent to England in 1915 declared medically unfit.[17] Since 1930, Ward had emerged as "one of the principal negro agitators in the UK" (as a Special Branch report from 1938 put it).[18]

The wider ILD campaign in Britain around Scottsboro was impressive and Braithwaite spoke at least four times in London on the issue, clearly establishing a reputation for himself as a powerful orator in the process.[19] For example, on 14 July 1932 at Trinity Hall, Poplar in the East End of London Braithwaite spoke alongside Ada Wright, mother of one of the Scottsboro Boys. The *Negro Worker* noted Braithwaite's speech:

> This comrade explained very well how this particular case only went to show how the capitalist class was spreading race hatred between white and black in order to disrupt the comradely solidarity between the working masses. He closed by stating that he hoped to see the united front of all workers, irrespective of race, colour or creed against the capitalist class – in their common class struggle.[20]

For Padmore, the recruitment of a militant of the caliber of Braithwaite must have been a reminder of how generally disappointing the progress of the CPGB through the SMM had been with respect to organizing among colonial seafarers. Padmore wrote that he "discovered when I visited Britain that there are so many Negroes there and some even in the Party. Yet not one has ever been sent over by the British movement" for training in Moscow.[21]

17 Featherstone, *Solidarity*, p. 70.

18 TNA, CO 295/606/4. For more on Ward, see the numerous references in Adi, *Pan-Africanism and Communism* and Pennybacker, *From Scottsboro to Munich*.

19 Sherwood, "The Comintern, the CPGB, colonies and black Britons," p. 158. In July 1933, Braithwaite would address a Scottsboro Defence Committee musical gala at London's Phoenix theatre. See Pennybacker, *From Scottsboro to Munich*, p. 49.

20 *Negro Worker*, 2/8 (August, 1932).

21 Sherwood, "The Comintern, the CPGB, Colonies and black Britons," p. 155.

In May 1932, at the first "World Congress of Seamen," organized in difficult circumstances in Hamburg, Padmore declared of organizing colonial seafarers that it "is the task of the advanced water proletariat in Europe and America to take the initiative of drawing these workers into their ranks and fighting their everyday battles." Indeed, Padmore emphasized "that it is the task of the ISH and its affiliated sections to give the Negro workers active help in breaking through the barriers set up by imperialist, terror and reformist treachery to strengthen their already existing organisations and to create new ones in the colonies." Padmore stressed the CPGB through the SMM led by Hardy must now do this work far more effectively.[22]

By 1932, despite the glorious inspiration of the "Invergordon Mutiny" of the Royal Navy in September 1931, which suggested the power to cripple the British Empire through militant mass action by seafarers from below was not in itself an abstract dream, the SMM itself was going through something of a general, almost existential crisis. In December 1931, at the Eighth Session of the RILU Central Council, Harry Pollitt of the CPGB had issued a strong statement against the RILU's insistence of the need to launch a new "red" union of seafarers in Britain on January 1, 1933. Moscow probably demanded this for reasons not unrelated to strategic interests in the Far East and the need to prevent the shipment of munitions to Japan.[23] As Pollitt put it, launching such a union would be "a crime against the whole of our work in England:"

> There are 2,000 members of the seamen's section of the Minority Movement in the whole of England [but] there are 146,000 seamen employed on British ships... we have these 2,000 members, 64 percent of which are unemployed, and most of them have been unemployed over a long period. We have not got in one dock in England

---

22 *Negro Worker*, 2/5 (May 1932), and "World Congress of Seamen," *Negro Worker*, 2/6 (June, 1932), quoted in Featherstone, *Solidarity*, p. 88. See also James R. Hooker, *Black Revolutionary: George Padmore's path from communism to Pan-Africanism* (London, Pall Mall Press, 1967), p. 26.

23 Henry Pelling, *The British Communist Party: A Historical Profile* (London, Adam and Charles Black, 1975), p. 70, and J. A. Mahon, *Harry Pollitt: A Biography* (London, Lawrence and Wishart, 1976), p. 174.

> a single ships committee. We have not got in England a single section of the seamen where we have a basis for a new union at this stage. Our fight is not a fight against the perspective of a new union, but our fight is against instructions being sent by comrades who have carefully avoided facing the fact and who propose to organise a new union for the 1st of January [1933].[24]

Despite Pollitt's protestations, the Comintern through the ISH transferred funds and support to the SMM leader George Hardy, a former secretary of the IWW, to begin preparation for forming just such a new "red" union. If the idea of "red unions" was deeply problematic at the best of times as even the RILU was beginning to realize by now, Henry Pelling notes that "the whole attempt to form a new red union [of British seafarers] in 1932, when unemployment was at its height, could not but be disastrous." A short-lived strike led by a minority of seafarers against wage cutting in early 1932 failed to stop the employers' offensive.[25] This led to widespread dissatisfaction among many in the SMM with its wider stress on forming a "new union" instead of trying to organize a united fightback through the NUS.

On July 11, 1932, the Comintern agent Richard Krebs, a former German seafarers turned ISH official and "Political Instructor," slipped into Grimsby from Germany to re-organise the SMM which, as a Special Branch agent tracking Krebs's movements noted, "from the Moscow point of view had been in a deplorable state for some time past."[26] Krebs's "mission impossible" seems to have involved trying to ensure the launch of a new "red" union of British seafarers according to the Profintern's schedule of January 1, 1933. As he put it in a letter to Albert Walter, secretary of the ISH, in September 1932 he aimed to organize a national conference of seafarers in Liverpool that December, and "at this national conference it must be resolved to form

24 Quoted in Morgan, "The Trouble with Revisionism," p. 148.

25 Pelling, *The British Communist Party*, pp. 70-1.

26 This is from the voluminous file Special Branch kept on Krebs. TNA, KV 2/1102/73a .

a new union."[27] In his infamous, sensationalized 1941 memoir highlighting the duplicity and ruthlessness of the Comintern, *Out of the Night*, Krebs recorded the three months in 1932 when he was active in Britain, attempting to enforce Moscow's will by any means necessary. Though Krebs's memoir is notoriously unreliable, there are few other accounts available from an agent at the heart of the Comintern which provide insights into organisations such as the ISH and SMM.[28]

> From Berlin, I soon received instructions to break Hardy and [Fred] Thompson [another SMM leader] with every means at my command, and to install a new leadership in the [SMM] *Apparat*. The methods of "breaking" men were as familiar to me as they were to anyone who had grown up in the communist movement. First I stopped all payment of subsidies. The *Seafarer* [a SMM publication] ceased to appear. One after one, the seven existing International Clubs in British ports were forced to shut down. Through unsigned leaflets spread among their own followers, I accused Hardy and Thompson of stealing workers' money and of complicity with Scotland Yard ... by way of revenge, Hardy denounced me to Scotland Yard, and detectives began to comb the East End, asking for a "Russian with an American accent..."

After just three months, Krebs was indeed deported from Britain in late September 1932, and so the RILU plan to launch a new red union of British seafarers in 1933 did not come to pass. However, Krebs recalled, "the campaign to break Hardy and Thompson was a complete success. The blustering Thompson was not dangerous; he was permitted to resign. George

27 See TNA, KV 2/1102/7b. This letter contradicts Pelling's assertion that Krebs "was sent to England to 'liquidate' the affair" of forming a new "red" union. Pelling, *The British Communist Party*, p. 71.

28 On Krebs, see Mike Jones, "Jan Valtin: A False Witness," *Revolutionary History*. 5/1 (1993), pp. 85-97, and Krebs's Special Branch files in the National Archives, in particular KV2/1104. Krebs's memoir *Out of the Night* was written after his break with the Comintern, under the pseudonym Jan Valtin.

Hardy was ordered to go to Moscow [...]"[29] Krebs also describes how as part of installing a new leadership in the SMM he tried to "break" an ally of Hardy, the leading black West Indian SMM activist Harry O'Connell, based in Cardiff. It seems O'Connell, a sailor originally from British Guiana who had settled in Cardiff in 1910 and now led a local organization there called the Coloured Colonial Seamen's Union, had apparently refused to submit to the levels of Stalinist discipline demanded by Krebs.[30] In private correspondence dated August 23, 1932, that was intercepted by Special Branch, Krebs in a racist manner attacked "the old Hardy disciples under the leadership of the nigger O'Connell (delegate of the world congress [of seafarers, in May 1932])." He described here and elsewhere how both O'Connell and George Padmore were apparently "old hindering elements" in the struggle.[31] A translation of his intercepted letter to ISH secretary Walter, dated September 3, 1932, reveals that Krebs had much to say in terms of colonial work in the SMM, or the apparent lack of it.

> We shall have to do pioneer work in this sphere as there is no colonial section in the N.M.M. nor in the Party [...]. In the formation of a colonial committee we must first of all get rid of all the old corrupt elements which hinder us in our work everywhere. George Padmore must be told

---

29 Jan Valtin, *Out of the Night* (London, Fortress Books, 1988), pp. 684-85.

30 Valtin, *Out of the Night*, pp. 685-87. On O'Connell, see Marika Sherwood, "Racism and resistance: Cardiff in the 1930s and 1940s," *Llafur*, 5/4, (1991), pp. 60-61, Featherstone, *Solidarity*, pp. 15-17, 94-95, and David Featherstone, "Harry O'Connell, maritime labour and the racialised politics of place," *Race & Class*, 57, 3 (2016).

31 TNA, KV 2/1102/7b. Padmore supported the "line" about creating a new "red" union, but seemed to allow a degree of flexibility and autonomy to local activists as to how this would happen. As Padmore wrote to Ward in March 1932, the ITUC-NW "is only interested in one thing, and that is – the SMM must organize the coloured seamen – not into any special Negro union, but together with the white seamen into one revolutionary union. This is our principle, which we will not compromise with. About the methods of doing this, we give you a free hand, we have no fixed rules for this." See Hakim Adi, *Pan-Africanism and Communism: The Communist International, Africa and the Diaspora, 1919-1939* (Trenton, NJ, *Africa World Press*, 2013), p. 146.

> distinctly that he must stop supporting these doubtful elements.

In the same letter, Krebs advised that Jim Headley "has not, in spite of several instructions, taken part in our work" and that Chris Braithwaite was another of these "doubtful elements." He had already taken action:

> We have expelled the negro Jones (London) who was formerly a member of the Central Committee of the SMM from the SMM and have also asked for his expulsion from the Party. Reasons: It was proved that Jones is working on commission from the N.U.S., that he gets his means of livelihood by lending money at fabulous interest to seamen (this he runs in connection with the N.U.S. bureaucrat, Marshall) and that he sells N.U.S. positions on board ships to seamen (negroes). This was all known for months but nothing was done. In an interview with Jones, he acknowledged that he had received certain instructions from a negro comrade in Hamburg and that these were not our concern.[32]

In his memoirs, Krebs alleged that "my presence in London was denounced to Scotland Yard," possibly "by the Central Committee of the British Communist party which *fiercely resented my high-handed intrusion into British affairs*," and accordingly he was extremely bitter, malicious and libellous about what he had to say about members of the CPGB, including Braithwaite.[33]

---

32 TNA, KV 2/1102/7b. The "negro comrade" Braithwaite was in contact with in Hamburg presumably was Padmore.

33 Valtin, *Out of the Night*, pp. 686, 690. Krebs even alleged that Braithwaite was an undercover Special Branch informant. "What I did not suspect, however, was that Comrade Jones had been for years, and still was, on the payroll of Scotland Yard." Such slanderous claims were typical of *Out of the Night*, and while it was published in America in 1941 and France in 1948, as John Mahon notes, "there were significant differences between the American and [1941 Heinemann] English editions of Valtin's book. A chapter on England comprising 18 pages in the American edition was cut to six pages in the English, every reference to English

Despite the attempt of Krebs to "break" Braithwaite, "Chris Jones" clearly remained a trusted and respected member of the CPGB throughout 1932. For example, in November 1932 he led a protest at the imprisonment of the British Communist and National Unemployed Workers' Movement (NUWM) leader Wal Hannington, outside Wormword Scrubs prison. As *The Times* noted, "the assembly was small and orderly and appeared to derive great satisfaction from the singing of the Internationale."[34] By 1933, through his association with the NWA and his tireless campaigning on behalf of the Scottsboro Boys, Braithwaite, the black seafarers' organizer, had struck up a remarkable friendship with the radical Nancy Cunard, great-granddaughter of Sir Samuel Cunard, the founder of the famous shipping fleet which refused to allow black seafarers anywhere near the decks of their passenger liners until the 1950s. Cunard was editing her monumental 800-page fusion of Pan-Africanism and Communism, *Negro Anthology*, for publication in London in this period. From November 1932, Braithwaite would serve alongside Cunard on the committee of the NWA, which also included Jim Headley and, from Sierra Leone, another colonial seaman Roland Ederisu Sawyer as well as figures such as Reginald Bridgeman of the LAI and the Trinidadian trade unionist Adrian Cola Rienzi.[35] In undated correspondence with George Padmore's partner, Dorothy Pizer, Cunard would later recall Braithwaite and Headley as both "magnificently intelligent and capable as well as very good men."[36] According to Cunard's biographer Anne Chisholm,

---

Communists still living including Pollitt and Gallagher, was also omitted." Mahon, *Harry Pollitt*, p. 329.

34 *The Times*, 28 November 1932. On Hannington's arrest, see Wal Hannington, *Unemployed Struggles 1919-1936* (London, Lawrence and Wishart, 1979), pp. 254-67.

35 Derrick, *Africa's "Agitators,"* pp. 283-4. See also TNA, MEPO/38/9/11a. On Sawyer, who like Arnold Ward had been interned during the First World War, see TNA, CO/295/606/4 , Adi, *Pan-Africanism and Communism*, pp. 282-3, and Featherstone, *Solidarity*, p. 90.

36 Quoted in Maroula Joannou, "Nancy Cunard's English Journey," *Feminist Review*, 78 (2004), p. 148. In 1933, Headley would return to Trinidad on Padmore's instruction and in 1934 help form the Negro Welfare, Cultural and Social Association. This would play an important role in the labour rebellions which would erupt in Trinidad in 1937. In October 1937, Headley would return to Britain to speak at an International African Service Bureau rally in London called

> the West Indian communist organiser Chris Jones was a friend of Nancy's at this time, and there were frequent meetings of black radicals at her flat. Nancy admired Jones's skill as an orator and political organiser and told [Henry] Crowder [her partner] that someone should subsidise him so that he could have a political career. Crowder was not impressed.[37]

Some sense of what might be called the "black internationalism" of the Communist International in this period comes out through viewing the photo taken of Braithwaite on a May Day demonstration in 1933. Braithwaite, from the Caribbean, is pictured standing on the streets of London alongside the West African activist H. Kwesi Oku, from the Gold Coast (Ghana) with an ILD placard highlighting the injustice meted out to Angelo Herndon, a black American Communist who had been imprisoned in Alabama for violating an old slave insurrection law while organizing an interracial relief demonstration.[38] This photo, with its African, American, Caribbean and European dimensions is in itself a striking visual testimony to "the black Atlantic" dynamics of radical black political organization in this period, and was just one of several photographs of "Comrade Chris Jones" published in Padmore's *Negro Worker* and reprinted in Cunard's *Negro Anthology*. We learn from Jonathan Derrick that "in June 1933 it was agreed, at a meeting in Nancy Cunard's house in London, to found an International

---

in solidarity with Trinidadian workers. See Adi, *Pan-Africanism and Communism*, pp. 274, 320, 322.

37 Anne Chisholm, *Nancy Cunard* (Harmondsworth, Penguin, 1981), p. 281. On meetings of black radicals at Nancy Cunard's London flat on 9a Heathcote Street, in May and June 1933, see TNA, MEPO 38/9/17a and TNA, MEPO 38/9/19b. Intriguingly, this flat would be the residence of C.L.R. James for most of the 1930s after Cunard moved out in early 1934.

38 On Herndon, see Robin D.G. Kelley, *Hammer and Hoe: Alabama Communists during the Great Depression* (London: University of North Carolina Press, 1990), p. 85. On Oku, see his critique of missionaries in H. Kwesi Oku, "The kind of Christianity we have in Akan and Akwapim districts on the Gold Coast" in Nancy Cunard, *Negro: An Anthology* (New York, Frederick Ungar Publishing Company, 1970), pp. 439-41.

Chris Braithwaite with H. Kwesi Oku holding an ILD placard in solidarity with Angelo Herndon designed by John Banting on the London May Day march, 1933

Labour Defence London Coloured Committee, with Jones as chairman."[39] Such meetings could attract up to thirty-five "persons of colour," including figures such as the veteran West African Pan-Africanist Robert Broadhurst, who had been involved in Pan-African Congresses organized in London in 1911 and 1921.[40]

However, after the rise to power of Hitler's Nazis in Germany in early 1933, in part as a consequence of the disastrously sectarian Communist party line which ruled out building a united front against fascism with the "social fascist" German Social Democratic Party, another great "turn" in the Comintern towards a new line was soon underway. Fearing military aggression from Nazi Germany, Stalin now moved to attempt diplomatic approaches to Britain and France for reasons of national security, and the theorists of the Comintern accordingly now sidelined anti-colonial agitation and increasingly drew a distinction between the "Democratic Imperialist" countries of Britain, America and France on the one hand and the "Fascist Imperialist" powers of Germany, Italy and Japan on the other.

---

39 Derrick, *Africa's "Agitators,"* p. 284. For the record of this meeting on 15 June 1933 meeting, see TNA, MEPO 38/9/22a.

40 Adi, *Pan-Africanism and Communism*, p. 266. On Broadhurst, see Marika Sherwood, 'Broadhurst, Robert (1859/60-1948), *Oxford Dictionary of National Biography* (2004).

This Communist turn away from encouraging anti-imperialist struggle against the supposedly "democratic" and "peace-loving" British and French colonial dictatorships in Africa and the Caribbean, and the CPGB's turn away from building militant rank-and-file trade union organizations such as the SMM and turn towards building the "Popular Front against fascism and war" would have profound repercussions for Braithwaite's involvement in the CPGB. As early as June 1933, both Cunard and Braithwaite, after an argument on the NWA executive committee with the NWA chair, the loyal Communist fellow traveller Reginald Bridgeman of the LAI, resigned from the committee.[41]

In August 1933, Padmore – while still editor of the ITUC-NW's *Negro Worker* - made what he retrospectively claimed as a principled resignation from the Comintern over their sidelining of support for anti-colonial struggle, and for his troubles, now faced a vicious public Stalinist witch-hunt. Black Communists like Braithwaite had to now take sides – either loyalty to Padmore or loyalty to the Comintern. It is a testament to both Braithwaite's own militant Pan-Africanism and perhaps also his experience of witnessing a Stalinist agent like Krebs at work first-hand in undermining the SMM that - unlike many others including Arnold Ward, who would remain in the CPGB for another two years – he decided to resign from the CPGB in 1933.[42] It was with Braithwaite clearly in mind that Ward in frustration reported to Communist officials that Padmore was sowing seeds of dissension "among the colonials" and "told [his] story in a way that comrades believe him still."[43] Though militant organizations like the SMM and ILD continued to be active for the duration of 1933 in areas such as Stepney, the loss of Braithwaite and the network of militant colonial seafarers he had around him was keenly felt by the CPGB. In 1934, Indian-born Shapurji Saklatvala, a leading CPGB member, complained that:

> Many things happen among the coloured seamen in the East End of London and members of the Party and of

41 Derrick, *Africa's "Agitators,"* pp. 283-4. For the record of this meeting on 9 June 1933, see TNA, MEPO 38/9/19b.

42 MacKenzie, "British Marxists and the Empire," p. 180.

43 Pennybacker, *From Scottsboro to Munich*, p. 85.

the unemployed workers' movement, living right in the locality know nothing about it, can give me no information and have no plans of even private friendly contacts or any desire to learn of the situation. There is a tendency to treat the colonial problem as a mere side issue and as nobody's business in particular.[44]

44 Quoted in Miller, Pennybacker and Rosenhaft, "Mother Ada Wright and the International Campaign to Free the Scottsboro Boys, 1931-1934," p. 395. For an insightful memoir of political activity in Stepney during this period from the perspective an ordinary member of the CPGB and activist in the ILD and NUWM, who resents the way such militant organisations were by 1935 wound up by the CPGB as a result of the Comintern's turn to the Popular Front, see Joe Jacobs, *Out of the Ghetto: My Youth in the East End, Communism and Fascism, 1913-1939* (London, Calverts North Star, 1978), pp. 116, 152-4.

THE COLONIAL SEAMEN'S ASSOCIATION

Aside from his independent networks of radical colonial seafarers, Braithwaite probably found his relative political isolation difficult to bear.[1] With a growing family to support, Braithwaite continued struggling to organize colonial seafarers with very limited support from the NUS. He remained involved with Arnold Ward's NWA, though in June 1933, around the time Braithwaite was breaking from the CPGB, Ward was stressing to Comintern officials the continuing importance of political work among colonial seafarers:

> Our forces is so scattered and so divided. But Scottsboro, Kenya, Nigeria, is beginning to make the Negroes think here. Color bar in the Seamen's Union, 100's of ships leave

---

1 Braithwaite remained in contact with Padmore and Cunard, though by 1934 both were now based in France. See Cunard's letter to the Nigerian nationalist leader Nnamdi Azikiwe in 1934, when the latter passed through London that summer. "Hope you will meet Chris Jones by now; make him take you to the docks where he works. A remarkable place. And he will also show you Walker's Café…unique of its kind." Quoted in Nnamdi Azikiwe, *My Odyssey: an autobiography* (London, C. Hurst, 1970), p. 197.

> the London Docks every month and only seven ships of this company gave work to Negro seaman a year. Stokers only coal ships oil burning ships the company will not employ Negro stokers in other profession such as music hall artists, 90% is out of work [...]. I could write you pages of hardships the Negroes suffer here.[2]

The period of economic depression had seen unemployment among seafarers increase, and as Marika Sherwood notes "between 1926 and 1934 there was a 19.4 percent decline in British, 40.5 percent in foreign and 14.4 percent in Lascar employment."[3] In June 1934 the NWA resolved that "the central task of the organisation" was "to aid in the organisation of the Negro marine workers in the metropolis and in the colonies." This might have resulted from Ward and Braithwaite arguing that such work remained more necessary than ever as there were no other organizations in existence willing to take it up in a serious manner.[4] His directly political work aside, Braithwaite also seems to have played a role helping black colonial seafarers, particularly Africans, find work playing roles as extras when necessary on the British stage and screen. However, though he knew Paul Robeson there is no record of Braithwaite appearing in a major role in any productions himself.[5]

---

2 Pennybacker, *From Scottsboro to Munich*, p. 48. Ward's grammar demonstrates the level of education available in British colonies to those outside of the elite.

3 Sherwood, "Race, nationality and employment among Lascar seamen," p. 236.

4 TNA, CO 295/606/4. The British section of the LAI had also always been keen to champion the cause of colonial seafarers, who, as they noted at their second annual conference "are subjected to the worst forms of humiliation, police terror and injustice." The LAI campaigned against the alien registration scheme and the NUS's support for the British Shipping Subsidy Act. See the Reginald Bridgeman Papers at the Hull History Centre, DBN/25/1, and Sherwood, "Race, nationality and employment among Lascar seamen."

5 His recruitment of black colonial seafarers for British productions would have been through his contacts with George Padmore and Amy Ashwood Garvey from the mid-1930s onwards. On the importance of black colonial seafarers for many stage and screen productions during the inter-war period, see Marie Seton, *Paul Robeson* (London, Dennis Dobson, 1958), pp. 38, 77, 99-100. On black theatre in this period, see Colin Chambers, *Black and Asian Theatre in Britain; A History* (London, Routledge, 2011).

He did however have a theatrical side, and did not shun directly cultural - or perhaps "counter-cultural" – work. His daughter Pamela recalls he once helped to organise a stage show in Elephant and Castle called "Blackbirds" to raise money for the Scottsboro campaign, a show in which he took a role in the chorus.[6]

In 1935, the new British Shipping Subsidy Act, which "effectively excluded undocumented Black British subjects from state-subsidized ships," passed into legislation.[7] This new attack on colonial seafarers was supported by the NUS bureaucracy. The Union published a memorandum to the "owners" in *The Seamen* on May 1, 1935, demanding that employment on ships should be restricted to "native British," "bona fide British-born" and "coloured British seamen domiciled in the UK." As Sherwood notes, the NUS leadership seem to have decided on "a campaign scapegoating cheap 'alien' labour, confounding the issues of race, nationality and domicile, and appealing to the jingoist tendencies in Britain." At the NUS' Annual General Meeting that year the Victoria and Albert Docks branch proposed a resolution demanding that the NUS slogan of "British seamen for British ships" should be expunged. It was ruled out of order.[8]

It now fell to Chris Braithwaite and the rank-and-file network he had around him to lead the wider defence of black and Asian seafarers. With the likes of the SMM and ILD now long defunct as a victim of the Comintern's turn to the Popular Front, on July 30, 1935, Braithwaite took the initiative to organize a meeting of twenty colonial seafarers at 68 East India Dock

---

6 Correspondence from Dorothy Rose du Boulay, 26 July 2011. Pamela dates this show as taking place in 1936, and notes Chris Braithwaite escorted one of the mothers of the Scottsboro Boys, Ada Wright, to it. On Lew Leslie's "Blackbirds," see Tony Martin, *Amy Ashwood Garvey* (Dover, The Majority Press, 2007), pp. 116-19, and for a review of "Blackbirds of 1936" at the Gaiety Theatre, London, see *The Keys*, vol. 4, no. 2 (October-December 1936). There was also a similar production called "Harlem Nightbirds" which played in London in June 1935 at the Grand Theatre, Croydon and then the Queen's Theatre, Poplar, before touring the provinces, a revue organised by Sam Manning, partner of Amy Ashwood Garvey – both of whom Braithwaite would have known by this time. Martin, *Amy Ashwood Garvey*, p. 137.

7 Tabili, *"We Ask for British Justice,"* pp. 78, 82.

8 Sherwood, "Race, nationality and employment among Lascar seamen," pp. 237, 239.

Road to resist this new attack. With support from still-existing Communist organisations such as the NWA and the LAI, this meeting decided to form a new organization, the Colonial Seamen's Association (CSA).[9] Impressively, from the very start the CSA embraced not only black colonial seafarers, but also other Asian seafarers, such as the Indian "Lascars." As the Indian Communist seafarers' organizer and future secretary of the group, Surat Alley, recalled, the CSA "started at the time when Italian Fascism threat[ened to] attack Abyssinia. The Association was the expression of the discontent existing among the colonial seamen and its aim was to redress their grievances."[10]

In early 1935, the murderous intentions of the dictator of fascist Italy, Benito Mussolini, to conquer the East African state of Ethiopia (then called Abyssinia) was declared. Liberia and Ethiopia were the last areas of Africa free from European control, its armies having heroically defeated Italy at the battle of Adowa in 1896. Since 1932 Mussolini had been preparing Italian troops for the proposed glorious resurrection of the "Roman Empire." In order to justify such nineteenth-century style empire-building, the ideology of "humanitarianism" was deployed by the Fascist regime alongside open old-fashioned racism. In time-honoured fashion, the criminal invasion and occupation of a sovereign nation was declared to be, as Mussolini himself put it, "a war of civilization and liberation."[11] Africans and people of African descent like Braithwaite were filled with both horror and rage at the spectre of Mussolini's Blackshirts spearheading yet another European imperial "civilizing mission" in Africa. Across the African diaspora an international

---

9 *Negro Worker*, 5/9 (September, 1935). According to a 1938 Special Branch report, the CSA was "founded as an offshoot of the L.A.I. in August 1935." See TNA, CO 295/606/4.

10 Marika Sherwood, "Lascar struggles against discrimination in Britain 1923-45: The work of N.J. Upadhyaya and Surat Alley," *The Mariner's Mirror*, 90/4 (November, 2004), p. 443.

11 The quote from Mussolini was from a speech he gave at Pontinia, 18 December 1935, quoted in *The Times*, 20 December 1935. See George Padmore, *Africa and World Peace* (London, Secker & Warburg, 1972), p. 153. Mussolini also defended his coming war with Ethiopia as a "civilizing mission" in an interview on 23 August 1935 with Ed Keen, the British United Press Special Correspondent. See *Daily Herald*, 24 August 1935. Padmore's *Africa and World Peace* has a useful chapter on Mussolini's Ethiopian "adventure."

explosion of protest now erupted, and Robert Weisbord has noted that "perhaps no single event in the twentieth century more clearly illuminated the nexus between diaspora blacks and continental blacks than the Italian-Ethiopian war." This was because of the collective memories Ethiopia evoked, with both "an impressive cultural tradition traceable to ancient Axum and a uniquely successful resistance to the European intrusion in Africa in the latter part of the nineteenth century."[12]

Robert Hill has drawn attention to how Italy's invasion of Ethiopia "marked the turning-point of nineteenth-century and post-war Black nationalism and paved the way for the emergence of an explicitly political Pan-Africanism."[13] On July 23, 1935, the week before the launch of the CSA, a new militant and political Pan-Africanist organization, the International African Friends of Abyssinia (IAFA), had been launched in London by the Trinidadian revolutionary socialist C.L.R. James and Amy Ashwood Garvey, the Jamaican Pan-Africanist and first wife of Marcus Garvey.[14] *West Africa* described how the IAFA launch meeting was "crowded" with '"men and women of African descent." The meeting sent "resolutions of sympathy with Abyssinians in their resolve to maintain independence" and began a fund

---

12 Robert G. Weisbord, *Ebony Kinship: Africa, Africans and the Afro-American* (London, Greenwood, 1973), p. 89. See also Rupert Lewis, *Marcus Garvey: Anti-Colonial Champion* (London, Karia, 1987), pp. 168-75; Mark Naison, *Communists in Harlem during the Depression* (Urbana, University of Illinois Press, 2005), pp. 138-39, 155-59, Cedric J. Robinson, "The African Diaspora and the Italo-Ethiopian crisis," *Race & Class*, 27/2 (1995), Robert G. Weisbord, "British West Indian reaction to the Italian-Ethiopian War: An episode in Pan-Africanism," *Caribbean Studies*, 10/1 (1970), p. 35, and Kevin A. Yelvington, "The War in Ethiopia and Trinidad, 1935-1936," in Bridget Brereton and Kevin A. Yelvington (eds.), *The Colonial Caribbean in Transition: Essays on Postemancipation Social and Cultural History* (Trinidad & Tobago, University of West Indies Press, 1999). The 1933 film *The Emperor Jones*, starring Paul Robeson, was banned in colonial Guyana in October 1935 fearing it would spread racial strife.

13 Robert A. Hill, "In England, 1932-1938," in Paul Buhle (ed.), *C.L.R. James: His Life and Work* (London, Allison & Busby, 1986), p. 69.

14 For a brief overview of the history of the IAFA, see Christian Høgsbjerg, "C.L.R. James and Italy's Conquest of Abyssinia," *Socialist History*, 28 (2006). This issue of *Socialist History* is devoted to the impact of Italy's war on Ethiopia in Britain. For a fuller account of the IAFA, see Høgsbjerg, *C.L.R. James in Imperial Britain*.

to either "send an ambulance" or "found a permanent hospital if there is no war."[15]

Chris Braithwaite at the same time as organizing the CSA now threw himself into work for the IAFA. On Sunday August 25, 1935, at a mass rally of the IAFA in Trafalgar Square, Braithwaite spoke alongside Amy Ashwood Garvey, C.L.R. James, George Padmore (who had just arrived in Britain from France) and the Kenyan nationalist Jomo Kenyatta, of the Kikiyu Central Association. This gathering resolved to defend Ethiopia from "the latest and most brutal example of European Imperialism in Africa" and demanded a lifting of the embargo on selling arms to that country, ""a wicked and deliberate discrimination."[16] As the *Daily Herald*, which featured a photo of Chris Braithwaite addressing the crowd, noted:

> Ringing cheers greeted the declaration of Mrs. Ashwood Garvey, wife of Marcus Garvey, the famous leader of the Negroes, that, "No race has been so noble in forgiving, but now the hour has struck for our complete emancipation. We will not tolerate the invasion of Abyssinia [...]"
>
> On the platform were the three young sons of the Abyssinian Ambassador, Dr. Martin, and beside them stood coloured seamen, students, actors, musicians, doctors and in, in his colourful costume and plumed headdress, a well-known racing tipster, waving the flag of Abyssinia.
>
> Every speaker was coloured.
>
> "We don't want war," said the chairman in opening the meeting, "but if Mussolini continues in his Imperialistic aggression, we shall rise like one man in all parts of the world, and we shall inflict such a disaster on Fascism that it will never be able to raise its head again."[17]

15 *West Africa*, 27 July 1935. See also Adi, *West Africans in Britain*, pp. 67-70, and Marika Sherwood, "Ethiopia and Black organizations in the UK 1935-36," *Black and Asian Studies Association Newsletter*, 43 (September, 2005).

16 See Hannen Swaffer's article in the *Daily Herald*, 24 August 1935. See also TNA, KV/2/1824/7a. See also Daniel Waley, *British Public Opinion and the Abyssinian War 1935-6* (London, Temple Smith, 1975), p. 115.

17 *Daily Herald*, 26 August 1935.

Chris Braithwaite speaking at a meeting against Italian atrocities in Abyssinia, Trafalgar Square, London, 19 April 1936.

Matthew Quest has suggested that Braithwaite was also involved in mobilizing his networks of colonial seafarers, which attempted to organize "direct action to undermine the economy and trade of Italy and smuggled weapons to Ethiopia through the maritime industry."[18] In September 1935, a general meeting of "members, associate members and sympathisers" of the CSA unanimously passed a resolution describing Italy's war on Ethiopia "an act of bestial aggression." The CSA declared "that wherever we are following our calling as seamen we shall protest against working in ships which we suspect are carrying munitions and war material for use against the Ethiopians and, if possible, we shall use our influence to prevent the delivery of such a cargo into the hands of the Fascist aggressors."[19]

In October 1935, Mussolini invaded Ethiopia, and given a free run by the major European powers and with advanced military technology, particularly aircraft, at its disposal the dictator of Fascist Italy had effectively declared "mission accomplished" by March 1936. Those Pan-Africanists with hopes that one country at least within the "white world" - the Soviet Union - might have mustered the necessary willpower to rally international solidarity with Ethiopia were to see them dashed, as by the 1930s the Soviet Union was inexorably spiralling down into counter-revolution. Leaving the major imperialist powers aside, the betrayal of Ethiopia by the Soviet Union, since September 1934 a member of the League of Nations, was particularly striking. As far back as October 1935, in an editorial "Soviet Russia aids Italy," the black American journal *The Crisis* had noted "the Soviets are raking in good capitalist profits selling wheat and coal tar to Italy for use in the war against Ethiopia." It branded the Soviet Union "opportunist" and

18 Matthew Quest, "George Padmore's and C.L.R. James's *International African Opinion*," in Fitzroy Baptiste and Rupert Lewis (eds.), *George Padmore: Pan-African revolutionary* (Kingston, Jamaica, Ian Randle, 2009), p. 122.

19 "Colonial Seamen warn Fascists," *Daily Worker*, 3 September 1935. See also "Colonial Seamen's Lead," *New Leader*, 6 September 1935. In Cardiff, harbour workers and coal trimmers apparently successful stopped the loading of coal on the Italian vessel *Rino Carrada*, while seafarers boarded an Italian steamer and "plastered her bulkhead with posters denouncing the fascist aggression." See Featherstone, *Solidarity*, p. 18.

their protestation of "defence of weaker nations" and "love for exploited black people" so much "flub-dub."[20]

When the news broke that the Soviet Union had sold oil to Mussolini, most of the last few black activists still involved with the CPGB and organizations like the League Against Imperialism broke with them overnight. As Padmore recalled, 'the few Africans in London who were associated with the League [Against Imperialism] through affiliated membership of the Negro Improvement [Welfare] Association, headed by Arnold Ward, a West Indian, severed their association with the Communists and helped to form the International African Friends of Abyssinia."[21]

However much heroic resistance the Ethiopians mounted to the Italian invasion, without international aid and modern arms, the odds facing them were insurmountable. While rebels did retreat to the mountains to conduct a guerrilla war, the Italians used poison gas bombs extensively to terrorize the rest of the population, even targeting the Red Cross and hospitals.[22] The mighty efforts of black radical activists internationally in solidarity with Ethiopia had been to no avail. As Weisbord has noted, "regrettably, the black world had the will but not the power to stem the tide of fascist aggression. Perhaps the greater tragedy is that the white world which had the power lacked the will."[23]

---

20 *The Crisis*, 42/10 (October, 1935). That issue of *The Crisis* also carried George Padmore's "An Open Letter to Earl Browder," leader of the American Communist Party, defending himself from the Stalinist smear campaign and denouncing the Communist International's political bankruptcy. *The Crisis* editorial was quoted in *The Keys*, 3/2 (October-December, 1935), p. 27.

21 George Padmore, *Pan-Africanism or Communism? The coming struggle for Africa* (London, Dennis Dobson, 1956), p. 330. For the rather sorry tale of one of the few Africans who stayed in the CPGB after the betrayal of Ethiopia, see Hakim Adi, "Forgotten Comrade? Desmond Buckle: An African Communist in Britain," *Science and Society*, 70/1 (2006).

22 Alberto Sbacelli, *Legacy of Bitterness: Ethiopia and Fascist Italy 1935-41* (Lawrenceville, N.J., Red Sea Press, 1997), p. 55. See also Piers Brendon, *The Dark Valley: A Panorama of the 1930s* (London, Cape, 2000), p. 279. The leader of a mobile Red Cross hospital commented: "This isn't war - it isn't even slaughter. It's the torture of tens of thousands of defenceless men, women and children with bombs and poison gas."

23 Weisbord, *Ebony Kinship*, p. 110.

The chair of the IAFA was C.L.R. James, the driving intellectual force of British Trotskyism during the 1930s.[24] James now played an important role in helping former Communists like Braithwaite, Padmore and Ward, who had all recently had their faith in the Soviet Union shattered, to re-orientate themselves politically. Many black militant activists were so understandably disgusted at the betrayal of the Soviet Union over Ethiopia that they began to retreat from radical and revolutionary politics altogether, and either turned to a purely cultural Pan-Africanism or fell back into lobbying and placing liberal demands on the British Government. There could have not been a better audience than these militants for James's anti-imperialist play about the Haitian Revolution, *Toussaint Louverture: The story of the only successful slave revolt in history*, which was performed in London in mid-March 1936 with Paul Robeson in the title role. James' timely invocation of the Haitian Revolution in *Toussaint Louverture* must have helped to counteract any tendency towards liberal anti-Communism among supporters of the IAFA, and in an important sense it symbolized the Ethiopian resistance to Mussolini on the British stage.[25] Though Braithwaite became very close friends and comrades with James from this period onward, the fact he did not now join James in the tiny international Trotskyist movement is revealing of Braithwaite's own shift away from revolutionary Marxism towards an ultimately more reformist form of politics after his break with the CPGB.

After Mussolini had declared his barbaric mission "accomplished" in 1936, the Emperor of Ethiopia Haile Selassie and his family fled into exile, arriving in London on June 3, 1936. Though Haile Selassie himself was, as Marcus Garvey put it at the time, "a feudal Monarch who looks down upon his slaves and serfs with contempt," the Ethiopian royal family were nonetheless warmly welcomed by thousands of Londoners as symbols

---

24 James was author of among other works a pioneering anti-Stalinist history of "the rise and fall of the Communist International," *World Revolution, 1917-1936* (1937) and a magisterial history of the Haitian Revolution, *The Black Jacobins* (1938). For more, see Høgsbjerg, *C.L.R. James in Imperial Britain.*

25 I am indebted to Robert A. Hill for this last suggestion. See C.L.R. James, *Toussaint Louverture: The story of the only successful slave revolt in history* (London, Duke University Press, 2013) and also Chambers, *Black and Asian Theatre in Britain*, pp. 94-98.

of resistance to imperialist war and fascism.[26] As *The Times*, a conservative paper not known for marking moments of mass anti-colonialist fervor, noted, "thousands of people were waiting outside the station to welcome the Emperor when he arrived," with banners upheld declaring "Welcome to the Emperor," "Well done Abyssinia," and "Down with Fascism and War." Amid the estimated five thousand people gathered outside Waterloo Station, the paper reported that "a little girl presented the Princess Tsahai with a bouquet of red and yellow roses."[27] This little girl was Chris Braithwaite's eldest daughter, Pamela.[28]

Late November 1936 saw the first annual conference of the Colonial Seamen's Association in London. Braithwaite, who was elected Chair of the CSA, "stressed the need of organisation as the one salvation of the colonial peoples." Surat Alley, who had links with the Textile Workers' Union in Bombay and the All-India Seamen's Federation, was elected secretary, while Braithwaite's old comrade from the NWA, the West African seaman Roland Sawyer, also served on the executive. The range of support for the organization was unprecedented and historic, as black, Indian, Arab and Chinese seafarers were employed in British ships in a very strict hierarchy of wages and provisions. This was a testament in part to the respect for Braithwaite's tireless work and dedication. As Tabili notes,

26 Colin Grant, *Negro With A Hat: The Rise and Fall of Marcus Garvey* (London, Vintage, 2009), p. 440.

27 *The Times*, 4 June 1936. For more on the remarkable scenes on Haile Selassie's arrival, see *Time*, 15 June 1936. The *Manchester Guar*dian noted "bright red banners were upheld by the Friends of Abyssinia organisation, and people were wearing amulets or enamelled badges in the Abyssinian colours or waving small Abyssinian flags. Many coloured people were in the crowd…" Indeed, "there was no red carpet on the platform, no festoons of flowers, no Cabinet ministers, no guard of honour, but there can seldom have been an occasion when the arrival of a foreign monarch so stirred the hearts." *Manchester Guardian*, 4 June 1936. The CSA was part of a delegation representing the black community of Britain which was spurned when it planned a welcome reception by Haile Selassie. See Robert A. Hill (ed.), *The Marcus Garvey and Universal Negro Improvement Association Papers*, Vol. X; *Africa for the Africans, 1923-1945* (London, University of California Press, 2006), pp. 629-630.

28 Bush, *Imperialism, Race and Resistance*, p. 222.

> attended by 51 delegates including representatives of the Negro Welfare Association, the Indian Swaraj League, the League Against Imperialism, the Cypriot Club, and the League of Coloured Peoples, the conference denounced the colour bar and the British Shipping Assistance Act, invoking Black seamen's and subjects' service in the Great War.[29]

The CSA demanded removal of "disabilities" imposed on colonial seafarers by 1935 Shipping Subsidy Act, which gave preference to white seafarers, and also demanded that "the seamen of the British Empire be given full democratic rights – the right to trade union organisation, freedom of speech and assembly." As Sherwood notes, "this was a great advance on the 1920s, when there had been no solidarity articulated between the various colonial seamen, and there had been no demands particular to their conditions."[30] In early 1937, the West Indian economist and activist W. Arthur Lewis praised the work of the CSA in the official journal of the League of Coloured Peoples (LCP), *The Keys*, noting it "deserves all the encouragement it can get."[31]

In late June 1937, Braithwaite was invited to address the fifth annual conference of the LCP held at London's Memorial Hall on "Britain's Coloured Seamen." He "gave a graphic account of the colonial seamen's troubles in this country."

> He said that the majority of the coloured people in this country were originally seamen, and that it is only through

29 Tabili, *"We Ask for British Justice,"* p. 159; Featherstone, *Solidarity*, p. 97; *Negro Worker*, 7/2 (February 1937). Sawyer, who in 1934 had joined the CPGB, was NWA secretary, and on his membership of the CSA executive see TNA, CO 295/606/4 and Adi, *Pan-Africanism and Communism*, pp. 280, 283. In 1939, Sawyer with Anne M. Bagshaw would write a play about students, *Colour Bar*, though it was not performed. Colin Chambers notes that "written on the edge of world war, its message is that breaking down the colour bar is as important in war as in peace, and this is linked to colonial self-determination." Chambers, *Black and Asian Theatre in Britain*, p. 225.

30 Sherwood, "Lascar struggles against discrimination in Britain," p. 443.

31 *The Keys*, 4/3 (January-March, 1937).

> want of work that they have been obliged to remain ashore and take up such jobs as they can obtain. He gave a distressing account of the life they lead, and specially of those who have children to feed. He mentioned that the question of the employment of coloured seamen was not so acute at present on account of the boom in shipping, but maintains that this boom will not last, and expressed a fear that as they were the last to be signed on, they would also be the first to be fired.[32]

Sherwood notes that "initially the CSA concentrated its efforts on the effects of the Shipping Subsidy Act: by late 1937 'the stringency of the application of the provisions of the Act was slackened,'" so "some success" could be recorded.[33] One CSA activist from early 1937 onward, the West Indian T. Ras Makonnen, born George Thomas Nathaniel Griffith in British Guiana, has perhaps left historians the most vivid description of the work of the group under Braithwaite's leadership. Makonnen described it as "a welfare and propaganda grouping," and recalled that since "we did not want a separate black union" for colonial seafarers, part of CSA work involved trying to persuade West African seafarers resident in Britain to join the NUS, despite all its appalling failings.

> They would be shown the weaknesses of staying un-unionised: that "if you do not join the union you'll always be paid lower wages by the bosses, and this will separate you from your comrades." Chris's role as leader of his "union" [the CSA] was to act as a mouthpiece if there was any injustice that needed taking up. He had his contacts with the Labour Party and with us, and if there was any case with, say, Greek shippers not paying some of these black boys' wages for nine months or more, he played an important role as a go-between. So he was looked on as a

32 Chris Jones, "Britain's coloured seamen," *The Keys,* 5/1 (July-September, 1937).

33 Sherwood, "Lascar struggles against discrimination in Britain," p. 443.

> leader in the same way as some of the outstanding Irish dock leaders in New York.[34]

If Braithwaite's internationalism and socialism found expression and flourished not simply in his leadership of the multiethnic CSA, his militant Pan-Africanism came to the fore in his key role as organizing secretary for George Padmore's new "International African Service Bureau for the Defence of Africans and People of African Descent" (IASB), formed in May 1937.[35] The IASB had been launched with the assistance of the Communist I.T.A. Wallace-Johnson, of Sierra Leone, a former seaman who was now secretary of the West African Youth League (WAYL) and a towering giant of African trade unionism.[36] In solidarity with the heroic arc of labor revolts which swept the colonial British Caribbean - including his native Barbados - during the late 1930s, Braithwaite repeatedly again took to the podium of Trafalgar Square alongside the likes of James and Padmore in early August 1937 and again in late June 1938.[37] The CSA also held separate meetings to discuss conditions in the West Indies during the labor revolts.[38]

---

34 Ras Makonnen, *Pan-Africanism From Within* (London, Oxford University Press, 1973), pp. x, 129. Makonnen's account confuses the name of Braithwaite's Colonial Seamen's Association with Harry O'Connell's Coloured Colonial Seamen's Union in Cardiff.

35 Padmore, *Pan-Africanism or Communism?* p. 146. For more on the IASB, see Polsgrove, *Ending British rule in Africa*. For a letter to the *Manchester Guardian* in 1938 protesting against British government plans to transfer African protectorates to the Union of South Africa from the IASB signed by not only Braithwaite (as "Chris Jones") but also George Padmore, Jomo Kenyatta, C.L.R. James, Lamina Sankoh, Peter Milliard and Babalola Wilkey, see "The Native Problem in Africa: European Imperialism," *Manchester Guardian*, 26 April 1938.

36 Peter Fryer, *Staying Power: the history of black people in Britain* (London, Pluto, 1987), pp. 341, 345. On Wallace-Johnson, see also Hill (ed.) *The Marcus Garvey and Universal Negro Improvement Association Papers*, Vol. X, p. 648.

37 *Africa and the World*, I/4 (September, 1937), and Hooker, *Black Revolutionary*, p. 53. On the rebellions, see for example Richard Hart, *Labour Rebellions of the 1930s in the British Caribbean Region Colonies* (Ceredigion, Socialist History, 2002). On the IASB and the Caribbean Labour Rebellions, see Christian Høgsbjerg, "'A Thorn in the Side of Great Britain': C.L.R. James and the Caribbean Labour Rebellions of the 1930s," *Small Axe*, 35 (July 2011).

38 See for example the CSA meeting held on 14 March 1938, mentioned in TNA,

Ever since the turn to the "Popular Front," Braithwaite together with James and Padmore also used to go to CPGB meetings to heckle and expose the Communists "pretensions at being revolutionists" by raising awkward questions about British imperialism.[39] As James remembered, they would speak about the struggles of French and British colonial subjects who now had been forgotten as Britain and France were declared grand "peace-loving democracies" and bulwarks against fascism. "While I would ask a question, and Padmore might say a word or two, it was Chris Jones who made a hell of a row."[40] In another interview, James recalled Braithwaite as "a very fine comrade [...] Chris would get himself into a temper and explode and make a revolution at the back of the hall [...] at the shortest notice, he could generate indignation at the crimes of imperialism and the betrayals of Stalinism as to shock into awed silence hundreds of British people in the audience."[41]

There is a wonderful portrait by Reginald Reynolds of perhaps the most famous "revolution at the back of the hall" ever made by Braithwaite, at a "Conference on Peace and Empire," organized by the India League and the London Federation of Peace Councils held at Friends House on London's Euston Road in mid-July 1938.[42] "The subject peoples are no longer docile and capable of being used to suit the purposes of imperial powers," Jawaharlal

---

CO 295/606/4.

39 By May 1938, the CPGB had retreated from offering British colonies independence and were merely committed to supporting interim democratic charter rights. See the May 1938 CPGB statement "Peace and the Colonial Question," discussed in Nicholas Owen, *The British Left and India: metropolitan anti-imperialism, 1885-1947* (Oxford, Oxford University Press, 2007), p. 244.

40 M.A.R.H.O. (ed.), *Visions of History* (Manchester, Manchester University Press, 1984), p. 269.

41 Socialist Platform, *C.L.R. James and British Trotskyism: an interview* (London, Socialist Platform, 1987), p. 6, and C.L.R. James, "Notes on the life of George Padmore [c.1960]," p. 36. This is an unpublished manuscript, a copy of which is available at the Institute of Commonwealth Studies, London. As James later recalled of Braithwaite's interventions at CPGB meetings, "he would intervene and say: 'You say that the bourgeoisie in India can make the revolution, but I have been in the Party and you have said that this was impossible. Comrade James, you have the document. Read out what they used to say.' I always kept the documents with me." See MacKenzie, "British Marxists and the Empire," p. 236.

42 On the conference, see Owen, *The British Left and India* and also the Reginald Bridgeman papers, Hull History Centre, DBN 27/3.

Nehru declared in his keynote address to the thousand-strong audience.[43] To reinforce this anti-imperialist message and so embarrass the conference organizers, mainly members and supporters of the CPGB, supporters of the IASB had secured the attendance and speaking rights of a "fraternal delegate" from the French Pan-Africanist movement, Émile Faure of Senegal, President of the Ligue de Défense de la Race Nègre (L.D.R.N.) and secretary of the Rassemblement Coloniale, an organization which united the nationalist movements of Algeria, Tunisia, French West Africa, Madagascar, Pondicherry and Indochina. According to Lelia Seleau, reporting the conference for the IASB journal *International African Opinion*, Faure's detailed conference speech demonstrated how "never, since the Revolution in 1789 has France given the vote to the colonial populations" as a whole. The French Popular Front government had re-established forced labor in West Africa, imprisoned journalists in Indochina, and arrested, deported and imprisoned a number of nationalist leaders in Algeria, Morocco and Tunisia. Seleau noted that Faure's address "came as a bombshell to those delegates who had made a vehement demonstration of their loyalty to the Popular Front."[44] Reginald Reynolds recalled that Faure "spoke with intense feeling, but used his time economically by delivering a broadside of ugly facts, relating to repression and exposing [French Communist Party leader] Thorez and Co." As the French CP supported the French Popular Front government, despite it presiding over imperialist oppression,

> Some Communists soon began trying to shout him down and Nehru had to call for order, but the disturbance was nothing to that which followed when I spoke myself. Some, at least, of the Communists realised that shouting down a French colonial delegate would do them no good

43 Pennybacker, *From Scottsboro to Munich*, p. 197.

44 Lelia Seleau, "The French Colonies under the Popular Front," *International African Opinion*, I/2 (August 1938). See also Padmore, *Pan-Africanism or Communism?* pp. 333-34, Reginald Reynolds, "Under Which King Bezonian?" *Controversy*, 24 (September 1938), Richard Seymour, *The Liberal Defence of Murder* (London, Verso, 2008), pp. 58-60, and Tony Chafer and Amanda Sackur (eds.), *French Colonial Empire and the Popular Front: hope and disillusion* (Basingstoke, Macmillan, 1999), pp. 20, 99-102, 163-66.

> among the waverers, whose views they hoped to influence. But with me they need show no restraint. I returned to the French delegate's theme, and began to elaborate it, but before I had been speaking for sixty seconds my attempt to state and elaborate simple facts was inaudible. The words "lies" and "liar" were all that could be heard until an immense voice boomed from the back of the hall.
>
> "It's the truth. It's the truth that yuh can't stand!" All the delegates seemed to be turning round, as well they might, to see who my champion was. And there stood Chris, like an avenging black angel. Once more I realised the dilemma of the Stalinists, for they relapsed into sullen silence, though not for long. I seized this brief opportunity to inform Nehru that the rowdies were not, as he might have supposed, fascists, but defenders of democracy and free speech […] Soon Nehru was appealing for order again, but I was hitting hard and when – for the third or fourth time – the meeting got out of hand there was another boom from the back of the hall. "Ah'm wid you, Boy," roared Chris above the tumult. And that, I think – for I was trembling with a mixture of anger and fear – is the most tender and grateful memory I have of Chris Jones.[45]

Reynolds, like his partner Ethel Mannin, was a strong supporter of the socialist Independent Labour Party (ILP). In 1932, members of the ILP had voted to disaffiliate from the Labour Party, which the ILP had been central to founding, in protest at the betrayals of the Labour Government of 1929-31 and had pledged themselves to building a socialist alternative.[46] The close links IASB members like James, Padmore and Braithwaite had with the likes of Reynolds and other supporters of the ILP ensured their uncompromisingly

45 Reynolds, *My Life and Crimes*, pp. 118-120.

46 On the ILP in the 1930s, see Gidon Cohen, *The Failure of a Dream: The Independent Labour Party from Disaffiliation to World War II* (London, Taurus Academic Studies, 2007), and for my review of this work, see *Critique*, 39/1 (2011).

anti-Imperialist argument reached a small but significant audience on the British Left, and clearly influenced many, including George Orwell.[47] Len Edmondson, an ILP member up in Gateshead during the 1930s, recalled in 1999 that Braithwaite, as well as James and Padmore all came up to address local ILP meetings. "He was a great character, Chris Jones. We had him at the Westfield Hall. He was a rough diamond but he was a very good chap."[48]

For the likes of Braithwaite and Padmore, their experience of the betrayals of Stalinism in the CPGB meant that they were reluctant to join another British left-wing political party. However, both worked very closely in firm solidarity with the ILP from the mid-1930s onwards, helping to organize the ILP's anti-colonial work.[49] For example, on Sunday, November 13, 1938, Chris Braithwaite spoke at Glasgow City Hall alongside Bob Edwards, former commander of the ILP brigade in the Spanish Civil War, at an ILP rally held to mark the 21st anniversary of the Russian Revolution.[50] Glasgow's "Red Clydeside" was an ILP heartland, which had returned four ILP MPs including the charismatic Scottish firebrand James Maxton in the 1935 general election, and ILP rallies in Glasgow could attract thousands

47 See for example Orwell's famous article "Not counting niggers" in *The Adelphi* in July 1939, republished as George Orwell, "Review of *Union Now* by Clarence K. Streit," in Peter Davison (ed.), *The complete works of George Orwell*, Vol. 11 (London, Secker & Warburg, 1998). For more on Orwell, see Christian Høgsbjerg, "C.L.R. James, George Orwell and 'Literary Trotskyism.'" *George Orwell Studies*, 1/2 (2017).

48 Interview with the late Len Edmondson on 21 May 1999, Beamish Museum, p 26. See the Len Edmondson papers, Tyne and Wear Archives Service, Newcastle, 4707/4a. There is a notice in the *New Leader* highlighting an ILP meeting with Braithwaite at Westfield Hall, Gateshead, on 18 October 1942 on "The necessity for socialism." See *New Leader*, 17 October 1942.

49 Padmore would even edit the ILP journal for a period during the war, and around this time the ILP paper the *New Leader* published a comradely and fraternal Marxist critique of the ILP as a political organisation by Padmore in order to allow him to publicly explain his reservations over joining. See George Padmore, "The ILP in the Past – and Now," *New Leader*, 12 December 1942. It seems likely Braithwaite would have shared Padmore's analysis of the ILP outlined in this article, though again their shared unwillingness to join the Trotskyist movement in Britain should be noted.

50 *New Leader*, 18 November 1938.

of people.[51] For Braithwaite to be invited to address such a rally alongside a national figure such as Edwards is testament to the high standing and regard in which he was held. As John McNair – who had also served in Spain with the ILP - noted of "Glasgow's Russia meeting" in his column in the ILP's paper, the *New Leader*,

> Bob Edwards and our coloured comrade Chris Jones both delivered excellent speeches which were much appreciated by the audience. Bob Edwards, of all our comrades in the movement knows the Russian position best, and the first hand evidence which he was able to give was of the utmost value. Chris Jones dealt with the struggle of the workers, white or coloured, everywhere against their Capitalist and Imperialist oppressors. These great City Hall meetings are being well attended, and good work is being done in getting the ILP message across.[52]

The IASB's relationship with the ILP and the wider British labor movement was then important, but what was more critical was that IASB helped ideologically arm and build solidarity with emerging black and colonial liberation struggles across the African diaspora. Braithwaite wrote a monthly column for the IASB journal, *International African Opinion*, entitled "Seamen's Notes." As Braithwaite wrote in an early issue in August 1938, he hoped

---

51 See Cohen, *The Failure of a Dream*, p. 41.

52 John McNair, "News from Somewhere," *New Leader*, 18 November 1938. Edwards, a former ILP councillor, had visited the Soviet Union three times in various capacities since 1926, and had met and had discussions in Moscow with leading figures in the Communist International at different points including Leon Trotsky, the Bulgarian Georgi Dimitroff and even Josef Stalin himself. On Edwards, who later served from 1943-48 as ILP chairman, from 1947-71 was elected chair of the Chemical Workers Union and from 1955-87 was a Labour MP in Wolverhampton, see Christopher Hall, *"Not just Orwell": The Independent Labour Party Volunteers and the Spanish Civil War* (Barcelona, Warren & Pell, 2009), pp. 136-145. On McNair himself, see Hall, *"Not just Orwell,"* pp. 61-5.

> coloured seamen, be they African or West Indian, take an interest in this journal and make it their mouthpiece [...]. We are living in desperate times and the coloured seamen have a great responsibility in helping their countrymen at home in the struggle for an improvement in their economic and social conditions. Those who sail between Europe and the West Indies can serve to keep their people informed about events and happenings in the various colonies and in this way serve as a link in uniting the struggles going on in all parts of the black world.[53]

Matthew Quest has summarised some of the issues raised within Braithwaite's columns, hailing him as "a voice of seamen that sailed between the United States and Caribbean, the Caribbean to Europe, and Europe to Africa:"

> Fighting to maintain workplace standards of a maximum of 12 hours in a 24-hour day, he also worked for unity to resolve the problem of workers from Portuguese Goa and India undercutting Black and white peoples' wages. Jones also condemns and exposes "the D[istressed].B[ritish].S[eamen] clause," a section of Maritime contract law which allows ships to leave European ports shorthanded, picking up extra workers in Africa or the Caribbean. This clause allows the shipping industry to pay workers of colour only room and board with no wages.[54]

Through his contacts as Chair of the CSA Braithwaite was also key to the distribution of IASB literature into colonial Africa and the Caribbean. As James, who edited *International African Opinion*, recalled, "we tried

53 Chris Jones, "Coloured seamen," *International African Opinion*, I/2 (August 1938). See Appendix A.

54 Quest, "George Padmore's and C.L.R. James's *International African Opinion*," pp. 121-122.

all ways" to get it into the colonies, where such subversive literature was prohibited. "We had one or two people who worked on the waterfront. They gave the pamphlets to seamen and people in boats [...] we got it around, to my astonishment and delight."[55] The contacts Braithwaite and others made in turn fed information and reports back to the IASB in London. James, for example, in his 1938 work *A History of Negro Revolt* describes how it was colonial seafarers who helped him appreciate and understand the mass appeal of the millenarian ideology driving many of the Copperbelt miners who took spontaneous strike action in Northern Rhodesia (what is now Zambia) in May 1935. For James, the "Watch Tower Movement" based on the "Revelations of St. John the Baptist" in the Bible and linked to the Jehovah's Witnesses, was a symbol of the coming African Revolution against European colonial domination. "It is difficult to say exactly the true influence of the Watch Tower. The writer has been informed by Negro sailors that its influence is widely spread throughout Africa, and that it is the most powerful revolutionary force in Africa today."[56]

In *Fight*, the British Trotskyist paper he edited alongside *International African Opinion*, James stressed just how important he saw the work of radical black seafarers in helping to foster international solidarity.

> Some of the African peoples, the Kikuyu of Kenya for instance, have representatives in London. Negro seamen live in London and can make contacts with Kenya and other parts of Africa. We can build up a real solidarity by fighting the cause of Africans, Indians, and other colonials here and by letting them know that we look to them to help us in the struggle [...] a revolutionary movement in this country can never achieve final success unless in close understanding and cooperation with the revolution in the colonies.[57]

55 Socialist Platform, *C.L.R. James and British Trotskyism*, p. 6.

56 James, *A History of Negro Revolt*, p. 83.

57 *Fight*, 1/3 (January, 1937).

One of the proudest moments of Braithwaite's political activism must have come in early 1939 when he was able to report news of the formation of a new African seafarers' union, the Sierra Leone Union, formed after the recent return of Wallace-Johnson back home to Sierra Leone.

> Through the initiative of Mr. Wallace Johnson, a leading member of the International African Service Bureau, a mass meeting of seafaring men was held at the Wilberforce Hall, in Freetown, at which it was resolved to form a union in order to protect and advance the economic interests of African seamen [...] the Union has enrolled over 1,500 members, embracing members of various tribes [...] the Sierra Leone Union should be an inspiration and incentive to the dock workers in other ports of West Africa, especially Takarodi, Accra, Lagos and Port Harcourt, to organise themselves in similar fashion.[58]

Braithwaite naturally also involved himself in struggles closer to home: despite a growing family of his own he would cook up rice and fish and then go up and down his street, Turners Road, making sure that those around him in the incredibly impoverished working class area of Stepney would not go hungry for two consecutive nights.[59] One *New Leader* columnist in 1939 noted that

> housing conditions in Stepney were, and still are, a blot on any society which calls itself civilised [...]. Bugs, cockroaches, beetles, bad drainage systems, small condemned houses, are the lot of the people, whose miserable existence is bound up with and directly a result of the society under which they are living. It was not so very long ago that it was my painful duty to watch hundreds of large cockroaches crawling from a factory on one side of the street into wooden houses on the other side. Children

58 Chris Jones, "Seamen's Notes," *International African Opinion*, I/6 (February-March 1939). See Appendix A.

59 Interview, Dorothy Rose du Boulay, 24 June 2011.

> and adults of Stepney had resigned themselves to the fate of living with vermin.[60]

Yet this was also a community of resistance, and doubtless Braithwaite played his part in all the local struggles against other local vermin, whether profiteering private landlords or the British Union of Fascists, who famously suffered their greatest defeat at "The Battle of Cable Street" in London's East End on October, 4 1936.[61] From late 1938 into the first half of 1939, for example, a series of rent strikes ranging from 2 days to 21 weeks swept Stepney, organized by the Stepney Tenants Defence League.[62] However Braithwaite always seems to have nurtured dreams of returning to America to settle there with his new family, on the grounds that England was "no place for coloured people."[63] Incidentally, Marcus Garvey, himself in London during this period, shared such sentiments. As Garvey put it in the late 1930s, "there is no employment here for coloured men [...]. I think America far better than England for the coloured man – the trouble is to get to America.'[64]

60 *New Leader*, 7 July 1939.

61 On the kind of working class struggles taking place in the East End, including fine descriptions of "The Battle of Cable Street," see Jacobs, *Out of the Ghetto* and Phil Piratin, *Our Flag Stays Red* (London: Thames Publications, 1948).

62 *New Leader*, 7 July 1939. The rent strikes are also discussed in Piratin, *Our Flag Stays Red* and Sarah Glynn, "East End immigrants and the battle for housing," *Journal of Historical Geography*, 31 (2005), pp. 528-545.

63 Interview, Dorothy Rose du Boulay, 24 June 2011.

64 Martin, *Amy Ashwood Garvey*, p. 139.

THE WAR YEARS

During the Second World War, Maroula Joannou notes that "black sailors in London lived mainly in the streets around the dockland which suffered heavily during the Blitz and worked not only as sailors but also as stokers, trimmers, greasers and engineers." We still know all too little of Chris Braithwaite's activism and experience during this period, but he remained in regular contact with Nancy Cunard, who interviewed this "West Indian friend of mine" in 1943 in order to compile reports for the Ministry of Information on among other matters the conditions of black seafarers in the Merchant Navy.[1] As Cunard noted, Braithwaite's work securing colonial

1 Joannou, "Nancy Cunard's English Journey," pp. 153-4. As Cunard wrote, "to these men from West Africa and the West Indies is due their full measure of national thanks. They have been to every one of the maritime war-zones and many have taken conveys to the Soviet Union where they have seen something of the rhythm of life of our great Russian ally." On some of the class struggles of black seamen during the early 1940s, see Marika Sherwood, "Strikes! African seamen, Elder Dempster and the government 1940-42," *Immigrants & Minorities*, 13/2-3 (1994). See also Sherwood's recent work, *World War II: Colonies and Colonials* (Oare, Savannah Press, 2013).

maritime labor during the war was a "vital urgency."[2] Yet as "Chris Jones," he continued to engage in public anti-war agitation. In June 1939, before the outbreak of war, and described as a "leader of Negro Dockers," he explained why, writing a searing article for the ILP's paper the *New Leader* on "Why the Colonial Workers oppose Conscription." Braithwaite here referred to, among other colonial injustices, the case of his compatriot Ulric Grant, who had recently been sentenced for ten years in prison for "sedition" after the 1937 labor revolt in Barbados.

> In the West Indies the elementary principles of democracy are denied the native masses [...] for example, when such savage sentences as ten years imprisonment have been given to the Negro worker Ulric Grant for championing the cause of his fellow workers, it is sheer impudence on the part of the British ruling class to appeal to colonial workers to help them defend their ill-gotten gains.
>
> We colonial workers have not forgotten the last world war, when all kinds of promises were made to us if only we would help get rid of the Kaiser and Prussian militarism. Hundreds of thousands died in Europe, Palestine and Africa. *But our masters have not fulfilled one of their promises.* Instead our reward has been more repressive laws, unemployment, starvation [...].

Braithwaite concluded by declaring that, for the colonial workers, rather than "allow ourselves to be used as cannon fodder," "the Imperialists' difficulties must be our opportunities to strike a blow for freedom."[3] He continued to speak out regularly at public meetings once the war was underway. For example, on January 29, 1940, billed as a "Negro socialist leader," he spoke alongside two Labour MPs, Reginald Sorensen and the pacifist Frederick Messer, at a meeting entitled "War! Why?" organized by North London Anti

2 Cunard, "On the coloured seamen in the Merchant Navy," p. 1.

3 Chris Jones, "Why the Colonial Workers oppose Conscription," *New Leader*, 9 June 1939.

War Council.[4] In August 1941, at the ILP summer school held in Bangor, Wales, Braithwaite spoke alongside Ernest N. McKenzie, a Trinidadian teacher and journalist who edited a new Birmingham based publication, the *Negro Citizen*, in what the ILP paper, the *New Leader*, described as "one of the most interesting sessions of the school."

> Chris Jones said that for forty years he has been a rolling stone in every part of the world and that he had yet to find a spot where under white domination elementary freedom is granted to the subject races. In the course of a description of conditions in Africa he made special reference to the Copper miners in Rhodesia, where for every *pound* received by a white worker the Negro receives only a *shilling*. At the conclusion of his lecture, Chris Jones paid a glowing tribute to George Padmore, "the greatest political leader of the Negroes in any part of the world." He associated himself with Padmore's declaration that
>
> "The problem of the oppressed subject workers is to free themselves from the domination of foreign Imperialism. The problem of the exploited white workers is to free themselves from British Capitalism. It will then be possible for white workers and coloured workers to associate in genuine fraternity and to move forward to the building of the socialist Commonwealth."
>
> The students left the session with a burning sense of the injustices suffered by the colonial workers.[5]

On December 6, 1941, Nancy Cunard paid tribute to Braithwaite's activism in a report to the *New York Amsterdam News*, describing him as "a good friend" of George Padmore and herself.

---

4 *New Leader*, 26 January 1940.

5 "Two Negro Leaders," *New Leader*, 23 August 1941. On E.N. Mackenzie, see Hakim Adi and Marika Sherwood (eds.), *The 1945 Manchester Pan-African Congress Revisited* (London, New Beacon Books, 1995), p. 141.

> Chris Jones recently spoke at a large meeting in Bradford, Yorkshire, on the Atlantic Charter, and on the reaction of colonial peoples to war – and to what is to come after it. Like many West Indians, a fine natural-born orator, Chris Jones has a big following for himself amongst the workers of London, and is making a big name for himself in England generally, as a fearless and just speaker.[6]

On May 3, 1942, Braithwaite addressed a "gigantic open-air rally" at the Downs in Bristol, held to mark May Day, international workers' day, which ended with a pledge of solidarity to "the coloured workers" and "all our brothers." As John McNair reported in the *New Leader*:

> By his striking description of conditions in the British Colonies, Chris won the sympathies of a crowd 1,000 strong, which was horror-struck that such crimes were committed in the name of the English-speaking race. Chris warned the workers of Bristol that the time was not far distant when the coloured workers in the British Colonies would take matters into their own hands.[7]

Later that month, the *New Leader* reported that Braithwaite also "addressed a very successful open air meeting" organized by the ILP against colonialism at "the historic 'Spouters' Corner at Wood Green" in London. Chris spoke alongside Don Macgregor, and "dealt with the mishandling of the Colonial Empire by the Government."[8] Testament to Braithwaite's complete lack of sectarianism when it came to making the case for colonial liberation comes from the memories of the veteran anarchist Mat Kavanagh, who recalled him speaking in London at the anarchist-run Freedom Press "meeting on India in the autumn of 1942." According to Kavanagh,

---

6 Nancy Cunard, "Article written for the New York Amsterdam News," 6 December 1941, Folder 1.3, Nancy Cunard Collection, Harry Ransom Center, The University of Texas at Austin.

7 John McNair, "ILP renews pledge of international socialism at great May-day meetings," *New Leader*, 16 May 1942.

8 See *New Leader*, 30 May 1942.

Braithwaite gave a memorable "description of the women of India who worked in the mines and on the docks. In terse, biting phrases he told of how the mothers soaked rags in opium for the babies to suck to still their hunger."[9] One gets some sense of the reputation he had established as a speaker by now on the Left that John McNair in the *New Leader* could excitedly note under a heading "Chris Jones on the Tyneside" that on October 18, 1942 Chris was "going North again" and was billed to speak that evening on "The necessity for socialism" at the ILP's Westfield Hall in Gateshead.[10] On February 26, 1943 he was again billed to speak on "Colonial Blacks on the move," this time again in London at the Freedom Press Rooms on 27 Belsize Road.[11]

As the war progressed, Braithwaite drew closer to Reynolds and Mannin, even apparently moving his family in with them at one point. As Reynolds recalled, he had never known about Braithwaite's family for years after first meeting him as "he kept his political life and name so well segregated from his job and domestic life that one never thought of Chris as having a family. He just never referred to it."[12]

> Then one day, in the middle of the war, a man whom I had sent to see Chris, thinking Chris could help him, mentioned Chris's children [...] I reported this to Ethel [...] it occurred to us that Chris had often visited us but that we had never been to his home and knew only one side of his life. It had never occurred to him, till we asked him about them, that we might be interested in his children. From then on [...] [Braithwaite's family] used to accompany Chris when he came to see us of a Sunday, providing us with some of the happiest memories of the war years. We, in turn, were occasional visitors at Chris'

9 Mat Kavanagh, "Chris Jones," *War Commentary* (October 1944).

10 *New Leader*, 17 October 1942.

11 *New Leader*, 6 February 1943.

12 Reynolds, *My Life and Crimes*, p. 120. That Braithwaite maintained his remarkable "double life" is quite incredible, yet the British state at least seemed to know of his true identity. One Special Branch file on the IASB dated 8 March 1939 noted that "Padmore remains in command, assisted by Kenyatta and Chris Braithwaite, alias Jones." See TNA, CO 323/1690/5.

> home, the great occasion being the christening party of a son, with George Padmore and Ethel in the unusual roles of God Father and God Mother, while I shared the honour by providing one of the boy's Christian names.[13]

Another rare glimpse of Braithwaite's political activity during the war years came in connection with the legendary Trinidadian cricketer Learie Constantine, also a long term resident in Britain and working at the time in Liverpool as a Welfare Officer for the British state. On July 30, 1943, Constantine and his family had suffered a racist indignity at the hands of the Imperial Hotel in London's Russell Square. Attempting to check into the rooms booked for him by his employer, the Colonial Office, Constantine was allegedly told the hotel did not want "niggers," and that he would have to find alternative accommodation.[14] The incident attracted massive publicity nationally, and as Reynolds recalled, Braithwaite made an intervention to ensure the wider black response to the affair was an overwhelmingly political one focused on smashing the color bar in Britain.

> Fleet Street - not conspicuously zealous about breaking the colour bar in those days – evidently decided that whatever you could do to black people as such you could not do to eminent cricketers. The hotel received some bitter editorial strictures, public opinion was evidently pro-Constantine, and when some Negroes from the docks demonstrated their views by heaving bricks, the following night, through one of the hotel windows, there was general feeling that

13 Reynolds, *My Life and Crimes*, p. 120. Braithwaite's youngest child was named Reginald George after Reynolds and Padmore. See Hooker, *Black Revolutionary*, p. 77, and Huxter, *Reg and Ethel*, p. 79. When he first saw the large number of children in Braithwaite's family, Reynolds, doubtless tongue in cheek, remarked to Chris that "I see you still believe in the tribal system." Interview, Dorothy Rose du Boulay, 24 June 2011.

14 See Gerald Howat, *Learie Constantine* (Newton Abbot, George Allen and Unwin, 1976), pp. 135-7. Constantine would take the hotel to court to win damages in June 1944. See also the discussion in Anne Spry Rush, "Imperial Identity in Colonial Minds: Harold Moody and the League of Coloured Peoples, 1931-50," *Twentieth Century British History*, 13/4 (2002).

> the hotel proprietors had asked for it. The brick-throwers were so encouraged by this manifestation of the sporting spirit that they took it for an encore and were organising some more bricks when they were gently dissuaded by a man known as Chris Jones. His own part in the story Chris modestly admitted to me some time later.[15]

On September 9, 1944, Chris Braithwaite died suddenly of pneumonia. The "rolling stone" had now finally come to a rest. This blow hit George Padmore in particular very hard. One friend of Padmore's from this period later recalled "the great pains he took to save the life of an old West Indian seafaring friend of his (I believe his name was Chris Jones) who was living in poor circumstances in the East End of London. He was deeply moved and stricken with grief upon his death."[16] "Padmore always felt a special responsibility for the family of this tough, cheerful, uneducated worker," becoming secretary of a committee to organize relief efforts to support Braithwaite's widow and find foster homes for the children, four girls (Pamela, Jeannette, Catherine and Sian) and two boys (Laurie and Reginald George). Other members of the committee included Ras Makonnen, Ethel Mannin, Reginald Reynolds and John McNair (representing the ILP on the committee).[17] As McNair stressed in his appeal for funds from ILP members in December 1944,

> Chris worked unceasingly for Socialism, in the ILP, in his work with sailors, and wherever he could work effectively. He was a good and a grand fellow-worker and comrade

15 Reynolds, *My Life and Crimes*, pp. 117-8.

16 Bush, *Imperialism, Race and Resistance*, p. 222. Padmore, "Chris Jones." Letter from Ambassador Subasinghe to James R. Hooker in 1964, quoted in Hooker, *Black Revolutionary*, p. 77.

17 On the relief efforts for Braithwaite's children, see Reynolds, *My Life and Crimes*, pp. 120-1, Makonnen, *Pan-Africanism From Within*, p. 148, Ethel Mannin, "Our debt to Chris Jones," *New Leader*, 10 February 1945, *New Leader*, 24 February 1945, *New Leader*, 10 March 1945, *Socialist Leader*, 30 November 1946, and "Chris Jones," *Socialist Leader*, 26 August 1950, the latter of which includes a photograph of two of his daughters, Jeannette and Catherine.

> in our cause. Chris left a wife and six children and a committee has been formed to give these little ones a chance in life [...]. Remember the Basque kiddies whom we saved. Let's do it again![18]

As Reynolds recalled,

> Ethel became treasurer of a small committee of his friends, which made itself responsible for raising money and keeping the children till they were old enough to earn their own living. Much of the money came in small but regular postal orders from poor people who either knew Chris or cared for the things he had stood for. Of all the funds with which I've ever been associated this was the only one that never, in all the years it lasted, threw the treasurer into a panic. When we were running short, a letter to the right person or periodical would always bring in all that was necessary for the moment.[19]

18 John McNair, "The Late Chris Jones," *New Leader*, 2 December 1944. See Appendix C. On the ILP's support work for the Basque refugee children who came to Britain – work which again saw Ethel Mannin play an important role – see John McNair, "A Great Task Accomplished," *New Leader*, 2 June 1939, and Hall, *"Not just Orwell,"* pp. 66-68.

19 Reynolds, *My Life and Crimes*, pp. 120-121.

CASTAWAY ON THE BLACK AND RED ATLANTIC

In 1925, the long serving president of the NUS, Joseph Havelock Wilson, had declared that "I have always believed that British seamen have done more to discover and establish the British Empire, and to develop it. It will be the task of the same men of the sea to keep it."[1] From the moment Chris Braithwaite arrived in Britain in the aftermath of the First World War up until his death he refused such a "task." He instead fought against almost impossible odds and in the face of the most bitter racism for black and white unity and an alternative, anti-imperialist and socialist vision for seafarers both in Britain and internationally, based on struggle from below. As David Featherstone has eloquently noted, seafarers' organizers such as Braithwaite "made an important contribution to processes which might best be seen as bearing on the decolonisation of the British labour movement," for "their organising practices shaped solidarities and internationalist cultures," and "shaped articulations of anti-colonialism which brought together visions of independence and a concern for labour grievances."[2] As well as forming the CSA, Braithwaite worked alongside the likes of Amy Ashwood Garvey,

1 Tabili, *"We Ask for British Justice,"* p. 81.

2 Featherstone, *Solidarity*, p. 249.

C.L.R. James and George Padmore to form and build militant and political Pan-Africanist organizations such as the IAFA and the IASB. As historian Winston James notes, the 1930s represented "one of the most crucial decades in the history of black Britain" as it witnessed "the birth and emergence of a number of new black organisations and a level of black activism that was unprecedented."[3]

Chris Braithwaite can be seen to have stood in a long, proud tradition of black radical thinkers with a deep connection to the sea, stretching back to the likes of the anti-slavery campaigning of Olaudah Equiano and Frederick Douglass. "You cannot write the bloody laws of slavery on these restless billows," Douglass once boldly declared. "The ocean, if not the land, is free." As Gerald Horne has noted, black sailors "were the tissue that connected the nodes along the so-called Black Atlantic," recalling "the tradition of those Black sailors who in the late eighteenth century had brought the word of insurrection in Haiti to the Deep South and southern Africa."[4] Paul Gilroy has noted that that "it has been estimated that at the end of the eighteenth century a quarter of the British navy was composed of Africans for whom the experience of slavery was a powerful orientation to the ideologies of liberty and justice." In the early nineteenth century, two Jamaican-born radicals, Robert Wedderburn and William Davidson, both one-time sailors who had experienced service with the Royal Navy, involved themselves in the early organized working class movement in Britain.[5] Among the London Chartist movement, the militant leadership of black radical William Cuffay is well known, but as Peter Fryer notes, Cuffay "was by no means the only black man who played an active part," citing for example two young militant black seafarers, David Anthony Duffy (or Duffey) and Benjamin Prophitt

---

3 Winston James, "The Black Experience in Twentieth-Century Britain," in Philip D. Morgan and Sean Hawkins (eds.), *Black Experience and the Empire* (Oxford, 2004), pp. 363, 365-66.

4 Gerald Horne, "Black Thinkers at Sea: Ferdinand Smith and the decline of African American proletarian intellectuals," *Souls*, 4/2 (2002), pp. 38, 39, 43.

5 Paul Gilroy, *The Black Atlantic: Modernity and Double Consciousness* (London: Verso, 1993), pp. 12-13. See also Peter Linebaugh and Marcus Rediker, *The Many-Headed Hydra: Sailors, Slaves, Commoners, and the Hidden History of the Revolutionary Atlantic* (London: Verso, 2000), pp. 321-322. Davidson was hung after the Cato Street Conspiracy.

(or Prophet), known as "Black Ben," who were arrested and deported after leading a demonstration through Camberwell on March 13, 1848.[6] Braithwaite's tireless agitation and organization among colonial seafarers played its part in helping to remake this radical tradition anew for the twentieth century in the aftermath of the Russian Revolution. At his funeral, black seafarers insisted on carrying his coffin from his home to his grave in tribute.[7] Just over a year after Braithwaite's death, in October 1945 the historic fifth Pan-African Congress took place in Manchester. There many of Braithwaite's old comrades in the IASB came together with many of his old comrades from the CSA to unite with many others, including black seafarers and the future leader of Ghana, Kwame Nkrumah, who had in his youth in the US belonged to the radical National Maritime Union. In Manchester, they renewed their commitment to the struggle for African emancipation.[8]

For Reginald Reynolds, Chris Braithwaite's impassioned oratory stood out in particular.

> At public meetings Chris was dynamite. At his best in the open air, where his tremendous voice scorned the use of a microphone, he would startle a crowd as much by his sudden vocal inflexions as by his blazing revolutionary wrath [...]. Thousands must have heard him speak, and should still remember him as Chris, who never knew his true name or anything else about him [...]. He felt passionately the wrongs of his own people in all parts of the world, he scorned the Communists as opportunists

6 Fryer, *Staying Power*, p. 239.

7 Information from Chris's daughter Pamela, 18 February 2014.

8 Horne, "Black Thinkers at Sea," p. 40. Those at the Pan-African Congress who had once worked at sea included Peter Abrahams (South Africa), Surat Alley (India), M.I. Faro (Nigeria), Rupert Gittens (Trinidad), I.T.A. Wallace-Johnson (Sierra Leone), J.M. King (Barbados), Ras T. Makonnen (Guyana), Ernest Marke (Sierra Leone), George Nelson (Ghana) and Kwame Nkrumah (Ghana). See Adi and Sherwood (eds.), *The 1945 Manchester Pan-African Congress Revisited.* The Cardiff-based Pan-Africanist Aaron Moselle highlighted the continuing injustice facing colonial seamen at the Congress, though the loyal Cardiff-based black Communist Harry O'Connell did not attend the Congress, as apparently he did not want to "affiliate with Trotskyite Pan-Africans." See Featherstone, *Solidarity*, pp. 70, 98.

> [...] and he had – as Ethel Mannin and I (among others) were to realise – a deep loyalty and affection for those white people whom he really trusted personally and politically [...] I loved [...] the rough, tough, honest goodness of him, and I was very proud of his friendship.[9]

Such a feeling was heartfelt among those who had had the privilege of knowing him and his work, as Ethel Mannin's testimony at the beginning of this essay makes manifestly clear.[10] Both James and Padmore must have felt particularly moved by the passing of this older, dedicated militant who must have in many ways represented their very ideal of an "organic intellectual" of the working class movement. As Padmore put it in his tribute to Braithwaite, "many were the working-class battles and campaigns in which he gave his best. He was well known in ILP circles as a fine speaker and agitator, and one of the foremost champions of the coloured race." Braithwaite's death was therefore "a great loss to the cause of the colonial peoples as well as International Socialism, the finest ideals and traditions of which he upheld to the very end." Padmore closed by predicting of Braithwaite that "his memory will long remain as a symbol of the hopes and aspirations of his race."[11]

It is not impossible that the memory of Chris Braithwaite was in C.L.R. James's mind when, while on Ellis Island facing deportation from McCarthyist America in 1952, he wrote his study on "Herman Melville and the world we live in," *Mariners, Renegades and Castaways.* James drew attention to the significance of one particularly striking passage in Melville's classic novel *Moby Dick* (1851), which celebrated the collective organization and struggles of the multiracial seafaring crew of the *Pequod* - the harpooners like Queequeg (a South Sea Islander), Tashtego (a native American) and Daggoo (an African). Melville's hailing of "mariners, renegades and castaways"

9 Reynolds, *My Life and Crimes*, p. 118.

10 Mannin would later recall in correspondence with Barbara Bush that Braithwaite was "passionate" about black disadvantage, gaining a reputation as a "fiery orator." Bush, *Imperialism, Race and Resistance,* p. 222.

11 Padmore, "Chris Jones."

stands, in its way, as a worthy tribute to Chris Braithwaite's tireless work as a "fighter for the oppressed:"

> If, then, to meanest mariners, and renegades and castaways, I shall hereafter ascribe high qualities, though dark; weave round them tragic graces; if even the most mournful, perchance the most abased, among them all, shall at times lift himself to the exulted mounts; if I shall touch that workman's arm with some ethereal light; if I shall spread a rain-bow over his disastrous set of sun; then against all mortal critics bear me out in it, thou just Spirit of Equality, which hast spread one royal mantle of humanity over all my kind![12]

12 C.L.R. James, *Mariners, Renegades and Castaways: The story of Herman Melville and the world we live in* (London, University Press of New England, 2001), p. 17. The passage can be found in *Moby Dick*, Chapter 26, "Knights and Squires."

APPENDIX A:
SELECTED WRITINGS OF CHRIS BRAITHWAITE

"Problems of Coloured Seamen"
Edited by Chris Jones
International African Opinion, I/1 (July, 1938).

From time to time I intend to discuss the problems and grievances affecting coloured seamen and invite the co-operation of all those who are interested in airing the disabilities of those who earn their living on the sea.

It might not be generally known that the number of seamen sailing on British ships from the United Kingdom is more than 200,000. Of these, Lascars or Indians number 48,000; foreign white seamen, 7,000; African and West Indian 6,500. Of the coloured seamen only the Africans and West Indians are members of the National Union of Seamen. This excepts the men serving in the catering departments, who, irrespective of nationality and colour, are not in the Union, as this section of the industry is still largely unorganised. Nevertheless, the Negroes are employed by the majority of British shipping companies only on tramp steamers or large cargo boats. Lascars and Goanese stewards are, however, engaged on some of the largest passenger liners, motor ships and oil-burners. This is because they are not organised, and in consequence are paid lower wages than Union men.

Scale of Wages

A comparison of the scale of wages between Union and non-Union men shows the tremendous savings which the companies make by exploiting Indians and Lascars. Negro and white firemen in the Union receive £10 2s. 6d., while Lascars are only paid £2 2s. A.B.s [able-bodied seamen] in the Union are paid £9 12s. 6d. monthly and Lascars £1 10s.

It is, therefore, no accident that shipowners like Sir John Ellerman, who controlled the Ellerman City, Ellerman Bucknall, Ellerman Hall, Ellerman Strick, Ellerman Wilson and other lines, died leaving the paltry sum of £30,000,000.

These benevolent shipowners who claim to be super-patriots, prefer to employ unorganised cheap Indian seamen rather than pay white seamen at Union rates. It becomes obvious that the Negroes who are in the Union have even greater difficulty in finding jobs, and are forced to depend on the dole. The only way out of this vicious situation is for the British Seamen's Union to organise the unorganised Lascars and Goanese and in this way force the shipowners to raise the standard of wages for these workers. But even here we come up against another problem, and that is the Colour Bar.

Divide and Rule

Colour discrimination is widespread in the marine industry, and it is exploited by the employers to play off one section of workers against the other. During my twenty years' membership of the Seamen's Union, I have often been confronted, like many African and West Indian seamen, with all kinds of racial chauvinism. Very frequently engineers would be willing to hire Negro seamen were it not for the objection raised by some white seamen that "If you take the darkie, we will not sign on the ship." But this is not the only form of racial discrimination which one comes up against. I shall have occasion to deal with other aspects of this question in future notes.

* * *

"Coloured Seamen"
By Chris Jones
International African Opinion, I/2 (August, 1938).

At this moment we, the coloured seamen, associate ourselves with the large number of labour organisations in Britain in condemnation of the ruthless bombing of ships by Franco in the Government ports of Spain. However, we blacks, unlike many of those organisations now protesting in this country, are not confining our protest to the bombing of British ships for we realise that we are very often able to obtain work on the ships of other nations when we are denied it on some of the British ships. Our attitude is dictated by our humanitarian sentiments, which knows neither race, nationality nor colour. It is quite true that while the ships of other nationals are quite prepared to engage coloured seamen, they do not pay the wages paid to American, Australian, British and Danish seamen. And it is for this reason that British coloured seamen, in order to maintain the high standard of maritime labour, do not generally go after such jobs. So we hope that in future British white seamen will not look upon their coloured union members, as a menace to their standards, but rather as allies trying to maintain the highest level of wages and conditions.

In the last issue of *International African Opinion* I appealed to every colonial seaman to get into touch with the International African Service Bureau, which is willing to take up their grievances and try to get them remedied through the proper channels. I again repeat this appeal, and at the same time urge coloured seamen to take a greater interest in their union activities. For only through their organised might will they be able to mobilise the support of the white workers on their behalf. I also hope that coloured seamen, be they African or West Indian, will take an interest in this journal and make it their mouthpiece. We are living in desperate times and the coloured seamen have a great responsibility in helping their countrymen at home in the struggle for an improvement in their economic and social conditions. Those who sail between Europe and the West Indies can serve to keep their people informed about events and happenings in the various colonies and in this way serve as a link in uniting the struggles going on in all parts of the black world. Coloured people, wake up! Let us unite our forces in the common struggle for our freedom.

* * *

"Seamen's Notes"
By Chris Jones
International African Opinion, I/3 (September, 1938)

This month I am referring to the case of the crew of the S.S. "Dover Abbey" who have been charged with desertion at the Thames Police Court on August 23rd, as this will be of particular interest to coloured seamen.

The eleven seamen who appeared before Mr. John Harris, the magistrate, comprised four Roumanians, three Chinese, two Estonians, one Moor, and one Portuguese African. The circumstances giving rise to the charge arose out of the fact that the original crew of the ship, who were all English, left the ship at Marseilles, even the Captain paying off. This ship is one which trades with Spain, and had been bombed by Franco's planes on previous voyages, and as it neared Spanish waters the crew and Captain thought they would prefer to vacate the ship.

At Marseilles a new captain was appointed, but he experienced great difficulty in obtaining another crew, and succeeded finally in signing on five at this port. He proceeded to Cette, where four more men were signed on, and two more later picked up on the beach and signed on by the master after the ship had gone to sea. These men understood that they would be paid off on arrival at the Port of London, an impression which had been given to them by the chief officer. Therefore, when the ship had docked they got themselves ready for shore. But the master, after consultation with the owners, informed the crew that they would have to take the ship to Cardiff before being paid off. The men objected, and walked off the vessel. They were arrested and charged.

Although these men were foreigners and not members of the Union; the National Union of Seamen, on a matter of principle, provided them with legal help, and Mr. Barnett Janner was engaged to defend them; and he did so very ably.

During the hearing, the Captain stated that the defendants understood the articles of agreement which they had signed, which was most obviously untrue, because with the exception of one, who had only a smattering, none of them spoke English, and four interpreters were employed in the Court. As a seaman I know very well that a captain never reads the articles in their entirety, which further disproves the captain's testimony. Although the judge, in his summing up, believed that the men were quite cognisant of the terms of the contract which they signed, he, nevertheless, thought it was their honest belief that they would be paid off at London. Taking into consideration the eighteen days they had been remanded to prison, he sentenced them to only a day's imprisonment, which meant their immediate discharge and repatriation.

Perhaps it is only just retribution that the "truthful" master of the ship who had brought the charges against the men, suddenly dropped dead a day before the case was finally settled.

* * *

"Seamen's Notes"
By Chris Jones
International African Opinion, I/4 (October, 1938)

Fellow Seamen,

For some time I have, noticed that even our coloured A.B.s have been complaining about the new system of working on deck. The chief officers of the various ships have been making it a practice to call upon the deck department to work at all hours. But bear in mind that no more than 12 hours must be worked out of an 24 in any one day. The main grievance among the coloured A.B.s, like that of the white seamen, is the so-called floating eight hours, which is optional with all chief officers. Nevertheless, they exact their pound of flesh. The remedy, however, is in the hands of the coloured A.B.s. Let them make their voices heard with the white A.B.s. Thus their union will be forced by their combined pressure have this anomaly righted.

Now particularly is the time for us to push forward our demands, for the past two weeks have demonstrated that in a capitalist crisis, all men, white and coloured, are more or less brothers. The dark workers, no less than the white, are needed to animate the wheel of "emergency." With the calling-up of the naval reserve seamen from the merchant ships, gaps would have been left in the marine service which the coloured seamen would have been called upon to fill. These seamen, who, in normal times find the utmost difficulty is getting jobs on any kind of ships, would have been able to secure work on any of big liners, where in the ordinary course of things, they would be allowed only as travelling passengers. Places would have been found for coloured seamen on even the famous Queen Mary.

It behoves us, however, to stick together and to do all in our power to go on those companies' ships which give us work during times of peace. For the super-patriots who will make the profits out of wars in which coloured workers have nothing to gain but further exploitation to meet the cost of the imperialist venture, would be using all their vast means and propaganda to secure the support of the coloured workers.

It is up to us, therefore, as coloured seamen, to enlighten fellow colonial workers during our travels, that we underdogs have nothing to gain by fighting in the interest of the imperialist robbers. This is a task which we must not shirk.

Fellow seamen, please send your ideas to our journal.

* * *

"Seamen's Notes"
By Chris Jones
International African Opinion, I/5, (November, 1938)

Beware of the D[istressed]. B[ritish]. S[eamen]. clause.

The recent case of a fireman from St. Helena, Magott by name, who was brought to London on one of the Union Castle boats, reveals the dangers of the Distressed British Seamen clause. This fireman was picked up at St. Helena by the S.S. "Garble Castle," running between England and South African ports. The Union Castle Company in particular is one of those which would sooner have their ships leave British ports shorthanded by several men, if it were possible, rather than give a coloured man a job, either on deck or in the engineers' department. If however; a boat is running homeward undermanned, it will, from necessity only, pick up coloured seamen from the colonies. It was in such circumstances that Magott was brought to London. On arrival he was paid off for the twenty-two days he had worked the ship, and then despatched back home under the D.B.S. clause.

Under this clause, no claim for wages is allowed, but a grant of 1s. a month is made in accordance with Board of Trade rules. Although not compelled to work, a seamen repatriated under the clause is induced to do odd jobs of one sort or another, "so that time may not hang heavy on his hands." In this way the shipping company obtains labour for nothing.

Coloured seamen, this is a matter into which we should look with more care than we have done in the past. Boats which would hesitate to sign on coloured seamen when they sail from London or Liverpool, show no such hesitancy in taking men from the West Indies if they are in need for hands to complete their crew. In some cases, as many as three or four men have been brought from such colonies as Trinidad, Jamaica, and Bermuda.

It is important that our sea-going brothers should pay strict attention to this matter and warn our fellow seamen in the colonies that under no circumstances should they sign on ships unless the Articles include the provision of wages for the journey to Britain and back again to their home port. Let them not heed the crocodile tears of the masters, when faced with labour difficulties in the colonies, and their plea to assist in getting the ship back to the Mother Country. If the Articles do not assure wages to their return destination, seamen should refuse to sign.

Fellow seamen, again we would urge you all to continue your vigilance by acquainting those of our coloured fellows whom you meet on your travels of the impending dangers which lie ahead of further exploitation of the coloured workers through the subtle methods of the pro-Fascist National Government, which has control of what we are assured is our Mother Country. Yet this same Mother Country, when it suits her, will show no hesitancy in delivering to us small pills from aeroplanes in order to strike terror among her children. The coming months will be very trying, and unless we are vigilant we may before we know it hear that some part of Africa is passed onto Hitler, who has learnt some of the humanitarian methods of our so-called Mother Country.

Again, seamen, please continue to enlighten us about your grievances, as this is the only open channel you have in which to express them.

* * *

"Seamen's Notes"
By Chris Jones
International African Opinion, I/6 (February-March 1939).

The most encouraging piece of news I have to report this month is the formation of the union among the seamen of Sierra Leone, West Africa. Through the initiative of Mr. Wallace Johnson, a leading member of the International African Service Bureau, a mass meeting of seafaring men was held at the Wilberforce Memorial Hall, in Freetown, at which it was resolved to form a union in order to protect and advance the economic interests of African seamen.

What is most significant is that the Union has already enrolled over 1,500 members, embracing members of various tribes, such as the Kroos, Mendies, Temmies, Susus, Limbas, etc.

The conditions among African seamen are terrible. The shipping companies operating between Liverpool and West Africa have been able to exploit them by playing off one tribe against the other, in this way preventing them from organising a united front in their common interests. In order to economise, cargo ships sailing out of Liverpool usually carry a skeleton crew of Europeans in the engine room. On arrival at Freetown the companies hire the African seamen, who are contemptuously referred to as "boys," to work the ship on the outward voyages and discharge them at this port on the homeward run. These deck hands and loaders, who are made to work at all hours and in all conditions of weather, are paid at the rate of about a shilling a day. Out of these low wages they are compelled to make "dashes" (gifts) to the headmen for the privilege of getting jobs.

I feel confident that the All-Seamen's Union will not only put an end to this shameful extortion but will agitate for such demands as: 8-hour day, a minimum wage, double pay for overtime, free company uniforms for boatmen, better and more food, improved sleeping accommodation and sanitary conditions aboard ship. I also hope that the union will strive to abolish the headman system and demand that the shipping companies negotiate directly with the union officials for the signing-on of men.

The Sierra Leone Union should be an inspiration and incentive to the dock workers in other parts of West Africa, especially Takarodi, Accra, Lagos and Port Harcourt, to organise themselves in similar fashion. For years Sierra

Leone was lagging behind, but now it has caught up and passed all the other West African colonies, thanks largely to Wallace Johnson.

* * *

"Seamen's Notes"
By Chris Jones
International African Opinion, I/7 (May-June 1939).

I must first thank those fellow seamen who, since our last issue, have sent us information about their conditions, which seem to be improving somewhat. There are still many grievances that require righting, but these will be removed only when you take a greater interest in your union. You can start by regularly attending branch meetings in your respective ports. Make your voices heard in the affairs of your union, for there all men are equal, and the greater your activity, the more chance you stand of securing your jobs.

The point I want to make just now is that all coloured seamen sailing on tramp ships must insist on being supplied with bed and bedding in future. They will no longer be obliged to purchase their bag of straw – their "donkey's breakfast" – and submit to the indignity of carrying it through the streets. For the companies, in agreement with the Union, have arranged to meet the demands of the seamen for the provision of sleeping accommodation. The new regulation is to come into effect in June, but it is up to you, fellow seamen, to see that it is enforced.

The National Union of Seamen, which is responsible for this concession, is taking a more militant attitude heretofore. So now it is up to us coloured seamen to get busy and show our white shipmates that we are willing to fight alongside of them for improved conditions, so long as they treat us as equals. Equal terms in an equal calling.

Continue to let us know your grievances, so that this journal can give publicity to them.

* * *

"Why the Colonial Workers Oppose Conscription"
By Chris Jones (Leader of Negro Dockers)
New Leader, 9 June 1939.

In the West Indies the elementary principles of democracy are denied the native masses. Therefore we oppose conscription. For example, when such savage sentences as ten years imprisonment have been given to the Negro worker Ulric Grant for championing the cause of his fellow workers, it is sheer impudence on the part of the British ruling class to appeal to colonial workers to help them defend their ill-gotten gains.

We colonial workers have not forgotten the last world war, when all kinds of promises were made to us if only we would help get rid of the Kaiser and Prussian militarism. Hundreds of thousands died in Europe, Palestine and Africa.

But our masters have not fulfilled one of their promises. Instead our reward has been more repressive laws, unemployment, starvation.

Just look at the condition of the African peoples in South and East Africa, in Jamaica, in Trinidad, in Barbados and other parts of the West Indies. Even a hard-boiled Imperialist like Mr. Lloyd George described them as "the slums of the Empire."

Furthermore, we shall never forget the shameful betrayal of Abyssinia by the so-called League of Nations dominated by the great democracies Britain and France.

We have no faith in Capitalist governments, regardless of whether they call themselves democratic or fascist. They are all Imperialists, and as such the exploiters and oppressors of colonial peoples. Therefore we are determined never again to allow ourselves to be used as cannon fodder by either camp in the coming war.

The Imperialists' difficulties must be our opportunities to strike a blow for freedom.

APPENDIX B:

OBITUARIES

"Chris Jones: Fighter For The Oppressed"
By George Padmore.
New Leader, 23 September 1944.

Left-wingers, especially members of the ILP, have heard with deep regret of the sudden passing of our esteemed comrade, Chris Jones on September 9th. His death is a great loss to the cause of the colonial peoples as well as International Socialism, the finest ideals and traditions of which he upheld to the very end.

Chris was born in Barbados, in the West Indies, 59 years ago, and started to go to sea at a very early age. As a seaman he had the opportunity to travel round the world. The world was thus his university, and what an education it provided him! It was always a pleasure to hear Chris, who was of a most gay and youthful temperament, relate his many sailor's yarns, and, in his more serious moments, to listen to him describing the conditions of the working-class in the various lands it was his good fortune to visit.

After the last war Chris settled down in London as an employee of the Shipping Federation, and since then he had always taken an active part in the working-class struggles of this country, especially those affecting seamen

– white as well as coloured. He was a member of the Seamen's Union, and every progressive movement concerned with the welfare of seagoing folk had his support.

I first met Chris about ten years ago. It was on the occasion of the mass meeting organised in London on behalf of the Scottsboro' boys, eight Negro youths who were being railroaded to death by American "justice." We were both speakers at that meeting, and from then a warm comradeship developed between us. Chris's participation in the endeavour to seek true justice for those Scottsboro' victims of class and race prejudice was typical of him.

He never spared himself in rendering aid to the cause of the oppressed. Many were the working-class battles and campaigns in which he gave his best. He was well known in ILP circles as a fine speaker and agitator, and one of the foremost champions of the coloured race. Chris was a member of the Executive Committee of the International African Service Bureau, the Negro Welfare Association, and several other progressive organisations working on behalf of the Negro peoples.

His death is a great loss, and his memory will long remain as a symbol of the hopes and aspirations of his race. To his wife and six children we extend our deepest sympathies.

* * *

"Chris Jones"
By Mat Kavanagh.
War Commentary, October 1944.

All revolutionary workers will share in our sorrow at the death of our militant fellow worker Chris Jones. He was well known in the North and especially in South Wales, and during the last few years, in London. The best coloured open-air speaker, he drew large crowds at the Docks among his mates. Being one of them, he spoke to them in their own tongue, and knowing their strength and their weaknesses, he knew just what points to make. The docker of today is very largely a disillusioned man; tricked and cheated so often by politicians and labour skates, he mistrusts the glib promisers who seek to get on his back. He is loyal to his own mates, and is capable of any sacrifice for solidarity. Chris Jones worked with them, took the same risks and paid the same dues. Always ready to fight their battles, his colour made no difference. His long and varied experience as a seaman enabled him to speak with authority of the conditions of the workers in all parts of the world. Those of us who can remember him speaking at the Freedom Press meeting on India in the autumn of 1942 will never forget his description of the women of India who worked in the mines and on the docks. In terse, biting phrases he told of how the mothers soaked rags in opium for the babies to suck to still their hunger.

Chris Jones left his home in the West Indies quite young and followed the sea. He saw capitalism at work under all conditions, and it aroused all his native antagonism to injustice and poverty. His was not an attitude of mere negative rebelliousness; he knew and always made it clear that there was no hope under capitalism; only by the overthrow of the present system could the emancipation of the workers be achieved, and that could only be done by the workers themselves.

His work amongst his coloured comrades made him loved and respected by them all, for these the true spirit of Internationalism shone out. His death is a great loss for the militant labour movement. His life is an inspiration and a spur to more energetic action, for he was a forerunner of the coloured workers who are finding their places in the International working class. The crisis is approaching; we must be ready for it, must take up the cudgels dropped by our comrades in the struggle. They have not fought in vain, there are willing hands to fight and keep alive the memory of the heroes fallen in the fight.

APPENDIX C:
APPEAL

"The Late Chris Jones"
By John McNair
New Leader, 2 December 1944.

Our readers will remember that our friend and comrade Chris Jones died about two months ago. Chris worked unceasingly for Socialism, in the ILP, in his work with sailors, and wherever he could work effectively. He was a good and a grand fellow-worker and comrade in our cause.

Chris left a wife and six children and a committee has been formed to give these little ones a chance in life. The committee consists of Ethel Mannin, George Padmore, Reg. Reynolds, Dr. Makonnen and one or two other friends. I represent the Party on this committee.

The immediate needs of Mrs. Jones and the kiddies have been attended to by the committee, but it is now necessary to start a fund so that we can carry on the work.

I know it only necessary to mention this in the *New Leader* in order to obtain financial assistance from those who have helped in the past in similar cases. Will any friend who desires to be associated with the work please send their cheque or P.O. to Ethel Mannin, Oak Cottage, Burghley Road,

Wimbledon Common, S.W. 19. Ethel is acting as treasurer and George Padmore as secretary.

I realise I have made similar appeals before. Let us not weary of well-doing. These children are coloured and they will have no chance unless we give it to them. Remember the Basque kiddies whom we saved. Let's do it again!

ON OUR OWN AUTHORITY! PUBLISHING
ATLANTA, GEORGIA

On Our Own Authority! Publishing (OooA!) is an autonomous research press in Atlanta, Georgia, founded in 2012. Specializing in anarchist studies and radical literature, we publish social movement history, post-colonial history, and studies of global political thought, emphasizing themes of anti-colonialism, direct democracy, and workers' self-management.

Other titles available from On Our Own Authority!:

Lenni Brenner and Matthew Quest, *Black Liberation and Palestine Solidarity.*

Joseph Edwards, *Workers' Self-Management in the Carribean.*

Emma Goldman and Alexander Berkman, *To Remain Silent Is Impossible.*

Sen Katayama, *The Labor Movement in Japan.*

Eusi Kwayana, *The Bauxite Strike and the Old Politics.*

Louise Michel, William Morris, et al., *The Commune: Paris, 1871.*

Kimathi Mohammed, *Organization and Spontaneity.*

David Weir, *Jean Vigo and the Anarchist Eye.*

Ida B. Wells, *Lynch Law in Georgia & Other Writings.*

Visit us online at www.oooabooks.org